Writing Through the Tween Years

Supporting Writers, Grades 3–6

Bruce Morgan

with Deb Odom

Foreword by Ellin Keene

Stenhouse Publishers
Portland, Maine

Stenhouse Publishers
www.stenhouse.com

Library of Congress Cataloging-in-Publication Data
Morgan, Bruce, 1955–
    Writing through the tween years : supporting writers, grades 3–6 /
Bruce Morgan with Deb Odom.
        p. cm.
    Includes bibliographical references.
    ISBN 1-57110-406-2 (alk. paper)
    1. Language arts (Elementary) 2. English language—Composition
and exercises—Study and teaching. I. Odom, Deb, 1954– II. Title.
LB1576.M73 2004
372.62'2—dc22   2004056580

Cover and interior design by Martha Drury
Manufactured in the United States of America on acid-free paper
10 09 08 07 06 05   9 8 7 6 5 4 3 2

For Ellin and Chris,
my friends, my mentors

Contents

Part III: Sanity in a Test-Crazed World

Foreword

met Bruce Morgan in March of 1981, in a cramped school office
south of Parker, Colorado. We had been hired as "overage" teachers—teachers to lower class size in a school with a burgeoning student population. The entire primary faculty and all of their students had
recently moved out of mobile classrooms to a new facility up the hill from
Northeast Elementary School. Bruce was to teach sixth grade; I had fifth.
The principal "resigned" within a month of our arrival. It seems he was
spending a bit too much time on the local golf course. The assistant principal was a warm, wonderful man who had absolutely no administrative
experience and our new colleagues carefully, but carefully, chose the perfect students to unload on the new, inexperienced teachers. Our only
interview question for the position had been, "Do you mind driving all the
way out here to teach every day?" We had signed long-term substitute
contracts in the superintendent's living room.

I believe Bruce's first words to me were something like, "Do you have
any clue what you're doing?" I was too terrified to respond. He thought
it best to discuss the situation over a beer or two—a policy that has served

us well any time knotty problems arise. I was twenty years old, technically too young to order my glass of red wine, but he was, at the advanced age of twenty-three, more than happy to order for me. Though he will argue otherwise, it really was he, not I who started the food fight in the teachers' room the third week of our employment (we were lucky it wasn't our last!). It was Bruce who picked me up every morning in his 1973 VW Beetle and, bungee cord holding the gear shift in place, drove us off to distant Parker to teach. We were gloriously rich—our starting salary was $11,352 and we couldn't imagine what we would do with all that money. And it was Bruce who suggested that my first classroom bulletin board, on which I had taped dog bones and written the words "Bone Up on Math" might be somewhat inappropriate for the fifth-grade boys in my room. I didn't get it. He gently explained. Those moments began, for me, one of the most significant friendships and professional relationships of my life. From him I have learned more lessons than I could ever recount here.

From the first moment I watched Bruce teach, I knew that, beyond being awestruck at his skill and rapport with children, I stood to learn more from him than I had learned in all the coursework I had amassed, all the professional books I had read. What he had to teach, no one can learn in a preservice course. He is my lifelong teacher and, as you read each of these pages, he will be, I've no doubt, the same for you.

Bruce's first lesson is about knowing each child. No teacher I have known has gone as far to learn as much about every student in his classroom, every year he has taught. Bruce's insights about students, reflected so brilliantly in these pages, are born of careful, knowledgeable observation, probing conversation, and an instinctive connection to children that is rare indeed. He knows his students academically, socially, and emotionally and in this book you'll learn how Bruce takes those insights and converts them to real direction for children's learning. When your teacher knows you that well, there's no way you're sliding by with work that doesn't reflect your potential!

Bruce's next lesson for all of us is that every child is capable of far, far more than he or she has ever been asked to give in school. The students with whom Bruce works have struggled in school from the beginning. They come to him as diamonds in the rough, longing for intellectual stimulation, hardened by failure, and anything but ready to learn. The phrase "all children can learn at high levels" has been overused and trivialized to the point that it has become cliché in this country. But Bruce breathes new life into the notion that teachers must have the highest of expectations for all children's learning. And by all, he means all. He goes far beyond the rhetoric in these pages to show the reader exactly how a teacher brings those words to vivid life in every action. In *Tweens*, we are given the opportunity to observe what happens to children who struggle when their teacher not only believes they are smart, but reflects that belief in every interaction with them.

Bruce also teaches, in these pages, that the genesis of effective teaching is in our own learning lives. Certainly he is not the first to suggest that what we ask our students to do must be for us first. He joins a long line of distinguished educators who implore teachers to read and write alongside their students not only to build empathy, but to focus on what is most essential for children's literacy learning. Yet, as I visit classrooms around the country, I must ask if we have fully heeded those suggestions. We are so pulled by the varying demands of our schools and teachers that we too rarely engage in serious writing in our own notebooks, reading books in which the ideas challenge our most fundamental beliefs. Yet it is through those activities that we come to understand what our children most need. For Bruce, as you will see in the pages of *Writing Through the Tween Years*, reading and writing are at once gifts, a source of joy, an indulgence, a colossal pain, and a significant part of a life passionately lived. I need hardly tell the reader that kind of spirit is contagious to children.

Our fourth key lesson in this book is that, in our struggle to balance the needs of our students, the demands of our schools and districts, and the call of life beyond school, we are not alone. With unblinking honesty, Bruce confronts the sometimes outrageous demands placed on us and guides us back to the reason we became teachers in the first place. With humor and a healthy dose of righteous indignation, he calls into question some of the sillier yet widely accepted norms in public schools and asks us to consider the much larger picture, beginning with the needs of the students we are here to serve. He hangs the dirty laundry for everyone to see, speaks directly with the elephant in the living room, and mentions the unmentionable in an unflinching effort to help us gain the perspective so needed in today's education scene.

As Bruce tells us in these pages, not every idea he shares is original. He stands on the shoulders of brilliant educators who have written before him. Don't we all? But, with spirit and ingenuity, he has translated ideas and tactics from other educators into the language of his own classroom. He holds some practices long accepted as effective up to the light of contemporary schooling and with the benefit of his experience, reexamines them, revises them and with a palpable freshness, puts them to work with his students. Will you learn practical strategies for use in your literacy workshop by reading this book? Undoubtedly. But don't miss the more important lesson: to teach with efficacy, passion, and virtuosity, we learn here that we must re-sculpt, reinvent the wheel, break what ain't broke, and challenge the conventional wisdom on behalf of our students. The voice you will hear ringing in your ears as you put this book down is a voice that implores us all to find our own path, our own inventiveness, our own ingenuity, our own best teaching selves.

Ellin Keene

Acknowledgments

It is nothing short of a miracle that this book actually happened. I have always been plagued with self-doubt and never considered myself capable of writing a book about what I do in my classroom. When Brenda Power e-mailed, and e-mailed, and e-mailed again that she was serious about the need for this book, I responded only out of a sense of politeness. I didn't think I had it in me; I didn't think that what I did in my classroom was worthy of written description. Honestly, when I talk about a cast of thousands, I mean it. This book would not have happened had it not been for the people who prodded, encouraged, and hauled me through this process!

The following people all had a role in making me confront my own securities, in allowing me to let go of the nagging suspicion that I was not "enough." You are amazing.

To Ellin Keene, my friend of twenty-five years, my inner voice, my mentor. You're always there, you're always consistent, you're always an advocate, and you're always on me to be the best I can be. You are consistently a voice of compassion and respect for education in a time when all around us are critical.

To Chris Schor, my friend, my conspirator. A model for what it means to face up to life, to deal with adversity, and to go on in spite of everything.

To Dawn Harbert and Barb Rohrer, for never doubting, for always laughing, for always nagging and pushing me to finish, for welcoming me into your classrooms and your lives.

To Deb Odom, for cutting through my wordiness and insisting that I actually put aside emotion to talk rationally! And for being as shocked as I at missed deadlines.

To Joan Banko, who constantly reminds me of our ultimate purpose.

To my fourth-grade colleagues, the dream team: Marla Applegate, Tami Coyle, Carolyn Ziegler. Amazing teachers, loving humans, and impeccable colleagues.

To my vertical team: Mari Everett, Julie Barton, Amy Benge. You love kids, bust them, advocate for them, and do all right by yourself at Happy Hour!

To Jason Kasper, for explaining politely for the twentieth time how to turn on the new computers; for actually believing that I understand the technology you're describing as I shake my head yes but know it's really shaking no.

To the kids in my classroom this year. Whether in the Glenwood Springs Pool, on the kickball diamond, or in the classroom, you always love, always feel, always welcome in others. You drive me absolutely crazy, and I love you deeply.

For Brenda Power, editor extraordinaire. You never wavered, (except that one day); for believing in me more than I did, and for being an education advocate. I couldn't have done it without you.

To Debbie Miller, always a model of civility and saneness in a crazy world. All I have to do is look at you and I feel calmer.

For Cris Tovani, who gives me faith in the high school experience.

To all my friends at the PEBC: For twenty-odd years, your thinking has guided my practices, kept me new and alive, pushed me to be more:

Judy Hendricks—the voice of reason, of organization, of gentleness.

Kristin Venable—countless lab experiences, and still you believe I'll pull it out and provide a memorable experience.

Diane Sweeney—that impish grin, that deep thought, that gentle push.

Chryse Hutchins—for seeing that beneath all the bluster and gruffness there was a gem somewhere. For that laugh of yours as you talk about all the things I swear I will never do.

Lori Conrad—who thinks the same as I do, acts the same, with the same raunchy humor and word choice, and actually gets away with it.

Mario—a voice of passion, of wisdom, and of cutting-edge humor at the high school level.

Carol Quimby—so professional, so wise, so full of student quips that surprise and delight. You are an inspiration.

To Liz Stedem—where are you? I miss you!

To my Scholars group and countless years of writing and black humor: Betty Bush, Patricia Cox, Sue Loftus, and Dana, who flew the coop!

To Rancer, my best friend of twenty-some years. You loved me even when you hated me and never waivered in your belief that I was "enough."

To Leslie "Becky Bob" Leyden—partner in crime, e-mail lifeline to the world outside the classroom, and cohort on Friday nights at Las Margaritas, where we would regain our sanity and begin the weekend.

To Randi Allison, for twenty years of beauty, oddness, and hilarity. You are the best, so giving of yourself, so accepting of those around you, so full of zany humor. Thank God you're out there!

To Janet DeFord—your sweetness, humor, drive, and balance serve as a model to me. Never crabby, always helpful . . . I don't get it!

To all my teammates at Castle Rock Elementary School—Our jobs are so hard, so challenging, and you meet the requirements with grace and dignity.

To my teammate of nine years: Sheri Kangas. Good cop/bad cop. Supporter of kids. Incredible parent. Visionary educator. Loving friend. You keep me focused, keep me realistic, and keep me from shooting off my mouth and getting fired!

To my former colleagues and teammates at Pine Lane Intermediate School. Luckily, we knew what we had when we had it and cherished the time and the relationships. There will never be a group like you again. Your passion, your drive, your sense of fun created an amazing place for our students and for us: Voice of Reason Shirley Gonerka, Not-as-young-as-she-used-to-be Caren Matteucci, Zookeeper Dan Erfurdt, new high school savior Pat McGuire, and Track A's more recent acquisitions—Lynn Napolilli, Jonathan Coldoff, Kristin Bernstein.

To Mrs. Remoh, who minimized road rage as my carpool partner and friend for all those years.

To Brent Kieft, for starting off every team meeting asking how we were doing.

To Danae Smith, for her gentleness, her ability to say no to craziness, and that laugh. For Karen Burns for being Karen Burns.

To my co-teachers who kept me sane and kept me laughing and focused all these years: Nancy Lauth and Claire Schieltz. It would have been the loony bin without you.

To Robin Stranahan, for twenty years of friendship, team teaching, and opportunities to push my literacy thinking.

To Libby Rife and Michelle Rooks, passion and creativity at the pinnacle. For having the courage to call situations as you see them.

For all my Cornerstone friends: beautiful Lu Lewis, who leaves you reflecting, Edna Varner, whose passion and humor see you through the darkness, to Martha Roberts for Two Truths and a Lie, to Rashene Davis for her writing about the "mean girls" down the block, to Sara Schwabacher, who can actually focus this group, to Suzanne Fraley for her gentleness and drive, and to Steve Prigohzy for assembling this amazing group of people. The work you do takes my breath away.

To Lalitha Vasudevan, for her constant desire for more and more knowledge.

For all my Shannon County friends on the Pine Ridge Indian Reservation in South Dakota. You are amazing: Bob, Angie, Monica, Marlene, Veronica, Karen. And for Babette, who repeated words thousands of times until I could pronounce them correctly.

For my Cleveland friends. You welcomed me, accepted me, pushed me: Anne Loftus, Nancy Zelenka, Kathy Francescani, Jodi Snyder, Mary Maul, and Tracy Martin. For Pat Faulkner who had every reason to say "Duh," and didn't! And for Downtown Janet Brown, who may just love Cleveland as much as I do. What a place. What a lake. What grand educators.

For my Bridgeport, Connecticut, friends: Judy LaChioma now residing in New Mexico, Cathy DiMenno, Lorainne Wojchik, Marge "Margemel" Cunningham, and Maria Miranda. The work you did! The work you do! Astronomical.

For Gary Debrizzi. For the courage to raise baby chickens in a classroom. For the courage to be a strong, gentle male in an elementary school classroom.

To my incredible brother and sister: Ron Morgan and Judy Brown, and her family, Tom, David, and Marky Mark.

For my mother, Juanita Morgan, who, even in death, was an inspiration.

To my dad, Donald Morgan, who hung in there and has provided countless stories that have entertained countless friends. To your recliner, "The Vinyl Resting Place." May it hold up!

For my friends who have passed before me. You were the beginning of my sense of self, my sense of history: Jeff Gibson, Earl Robinson, Dick "Fergy" Ferguson, and Tom.

For my former teachers who put up with me: Mrs. Cook, Mrs. Mann, Mrs. Pearson, Mrs. Aielo, and Mrs. Wedding. I actually made it.

For Florie Lehrburger, for coaching me through all of this!

For Miss Taylor, for making me read and for introducing me to the world of books when all others had given up.

For my dogs, Gladys and Cody, source of endless stories.

I did it.

Introduction

Just let me say right off the bat, it was a bike accident.

It was about as "accidental" as you can get, too.

Like Mick wasn't riding crazy. Or dodging in and out of traffic. And both of his hands were on the handlebars and all like that.

His tire just hit a rock. And he skidded into the back of a passing truck. And that was that. There wasn't a scratch on him. It was a head injury. Period.

So this isn't the kind of book where you meet the main character and you get to like him real well and then he dies at the end. I hate that kind of book. And besides, I can't think of anything worse than using my brother's accident as the tear-jerking climax to some tragic story.

I don't want to make you cry.

I just want to tell you about Mick.

But I thought you should know right up front that he's not here anymore.

I just thought that would be fair.

Barbara Park, *Mick Harte Was Here*

*J*ust like in one of my favorite novels, *Mick Harte Was Here*, I wanted to let you know right here and now what this book is and what it is not. I want you to know right up front what to expect, what I'm setting out to achieve, and what I'm thinking. *I just thought that would be fair.*

This book isn't about slick writing workshops where everything flows and goes smoothly. It's about daily struggles, questions, successes, and effective teaching practices. It's about classrooms and kids like yours.

The impetus for writing this book was our state testing program. My colleagues and I felt we had begun to teach to the test instead of teaching effectively. The sad part was that our writing scores weren't going up as a result of test preparation madness.

We had to take a hard look at our practices and face our fears that we weren't good enough or didn't know enough to be teaching writing well. It's not easy having confidence as a teacher in these times. It's hard to be secure in such an insecure political climate.

Let Every Child Be Assessed!

One afternoon a few years ago Dawn Harbert, Barb Rohrer, Deb Odom, and I were busily completing one of our sixth-grade student assessments for the district. This meant administering a reading inventory for each student individually, and the results would be placed in their permanent files. It was only Wednesday, but it already felt like Friday. All week we had camped out in the hallway as we pulled kid after kid to read and respond. When finished, like good McDonald's employees, we'd holler into the room, "NEXT!" Every ten minutes or so, we'd also yell, "You need to stay busy in there and be on task!" Every so often, a small voice would waft out the door, "Are you ever coming back?" to which we'd reply, "Probably not!"

Each assessment took approximately twenty minutes, but we were supposed to take each student to the frustration level, which could take up to an hour per student. We had twenty-seven to twenty-nine kids in each classroom, which translated into nine to twenty-seven hours of assessment per class; and that was before we filled out the paperwork for the district, entered it on their data sheets, filled out the Individual Learning Plan information, and filed the paperwork in the Body of Evidence folders.

This is in addition to nine hours of state testing each year. We administer running records on kids as needed and throw in additional computer reading tests of randomly selected students. Arrrrgh!

That afternoon, sitting in the lounge, Dawn began, "You know, this is why we hear comments in the lounge like, 'It used to be so much fun to teach!'"

"Remember the good old days when January through March was prime teaching time? Now all we do is test!" Barb added. "I still love the kids, but I'm thinking of retiring early; it just isn't worth the pressure anymore."

Deb, always scientific, stated, "You know, we're assessment junkies. We're so busy testing and assessing that we have little time to evaluate the assessments to see what we should be teaching!"

Our conversation escalated as we rehashed more testing frustrations. It seemed that nothing mattered but the results on our Colorado state assessment program, the CSAP. The CSAP results seemed to validate or invalidate what we had worked on for the year. It didn't matter if students had been successful analyzing text structures of historic fiction, researched an event from history, and written historic fiction. It didn't matter if they had researched writing style elements of Jean Craighead George or Avi and Scott O'Dell, and then mimicked their style. It all boiled down to the scores on the state reading and writing tests.

We talked about the way the testing pits teacher against teacher and draws into question your teaching philosophy. Back-to-basics teachers are pitted against process-oriented teachers. When testing results come back, you immediately check to see where your school ranks in relation to other schools in the district. You either feel shame or you celebrate. Then, you get nervous. You compare your class to the other classes at the same grade level. Of course, you want your class to score high, to prove that you're an effective teacher, to prove your philosophy works with your students.

As we talked, it was obvious that our real frustration was not the testing. We had compromised our teaching in the name of the tests. We were bowing to the pressure to raise scores instead of using assessment to determine what needed to be taught.

In the process, we had forgotten what was important—to teach. To teach well. We had forgotten it was our job to accept twenty-seven individual students exactly where they were in their reading and writing and then say, "Okay, let's see how far we can go!" We had forgotten that our job was to know our students as people and to honor their struggles and growth.

Nowhere was it more obvious how much we had compromised our teaching than in our writing workshops. In the name of higher test scores, we had given away our student-centered curriculum and replaced it with prescribed writing activities and formulas for good writing. Initially, these programs raised our test scores, but then they began to fall again. And, in the process of teaching the three-sentence paragraphs and transition clauses, many of our writers began to lose their voice. We were having students write to too many prompts and, in the process, losing a sense of who our writers were as humans. We were encouraging too many short pieces to be completed in a two-day cycle to mimic the state testing protocol. The formulaic writing and test prep had killed our writing workshops, killed our passion, and killed the enthusiasm and voices of our students.

We pledged to teach again—to put aside the test pressure and put the pressure back on teaching effectively, on conferring with students and assessing their writing to determine the next teaching steps for them as individuals and for the class as a whole.

We formed an emotional football huddle and did everything but yell, "LET'S GO!" Where was the pep band when you needed them?

Reality did, of course, set in.

I hate that.

If we were going to "Just Say No to Formula Writing and Test Prep," we had to know what we wanted to be doing instead. We needed to understand our philosophy—what we were going to teach and why. We had a responsibility to keep scores up while we actually taught—a responsibility to ourselves, to the kids, to the community and school, and to our principal, who stands on the firing line for us.

Over the next few weeks, we met after school to detail our list of non-negotiables. Our list included writing in different genres after researching text features and essential elements of those genres. We knew we needed to study effectively written mentor pieces in reading. We wanted mentor writers we could mimic, and we wanted to have excellent examples of their work at our fingertips. We wanted students to write deeply about small situations.

More writing topics needed to be selected by students. The students needed real audiences and real purposes for their writing. They needed feedback on what was effective and directions for the next steps.

Looking for wisdom from our heroes, we pored through Lucy Calkins, Ralph Fletcher, Katie Wood Ray, Regie Routman, and Joanne

Hindley. Everything we read verified that we were right in what we wanted for our kids, and for ourselves.

Assessment would be vital to our writing program, but the assessments would not drive our instruction. We would confer with our students, making notes about next teaching steps and would determine if those steps warranted whole-class crafting lessons, individual conferences, or small groups of writers with the same need. Writing prompts would be scored using a standard assessment rubric. However, we'd use those results to determine our next teaching points.

Ellin Keene and other friends at Public Education and Business Coalition (PEBC), a nonprofit organization dedicated to improving instruction in our public schools, have always maintained that kids will do well if they are taught well. They believe kids need to study test taking as a genre. This testing genre study should take two weeks, prior to the state testing.

Lucy Calkins, in her book *A Teacher's Guide to Standardized Reading Tests* (1998), quotes many research sources, all pointing to the same bottom line—kids who are in constructivist, literature-based classrooms do better on *reading* tests. Why wouldn't this also apply to writing? It just makes sense.

State testing and federal mandates are a part of our lives, just as they are part of yours, and it is up to us to deal with the challenges they pose.

I'm still in charge of the learning in my classroom. I know that it is my obligation to my kids and to my values to speak up and advocate for my students; they need me to do this. It is my job to minimize the classroom disruptions that plague us, and to accept that which I cannot change and change that which I can. I can't change the testing. I'm not a victim, however, and I can change the weight and the scope of that testing in my classroom.

Organization of This Book

The process of writing this book began with the help of incredible third-through sixth-grade teachers at Castle Rock Elementary School in Colorado. Our collective concerns, questions, and nagging doubts prompted our reflection on our thinking, our philosophy, and our classroom practices. We wanted our classrooms to be places that created great thinkers and writers who could use language to communicate clearly, classrooms that were tailored to the needs of kids in the intermediate years.

Much is written about primary classrooms, primary theory, and primary kids. This book is about kids who are often forgotten in professional books on teaching, kids in between primary grades and middle schools. Advertisers and sociologists call this group of kids "tweens"—kids in between being a child and a teenager.

This book has as its core nagging issues facing teachers of the tween writers. Some of the concerns and nagging issues I investigate, which may be yours as well, are:

* What are the special needs of students during the tween years?
* What does a typical writers' workshop look like, and how do we fit in all that we're expected to do?
* What is essential for creating a safe environment for kids to do their best writing?
* What is a healthy balance between test preparation and rigorous teaching, between test preparation and student choice?
* How do we demonstrate most effectively what we know and encourage our kids to take risks with their writing in regard to content and conventions of print?
* How do we get kids to internalize quality standards and write effectively, using the tools we have demonstrated?

It is my chance to convey what we have tried in our school and specifically what happens in my classroom. My job is to share what works for me.

The three parts of this book address many of these questions.

Part One, Writing Essentials, is about setting up writing programs to work with tween writers. I look at the lives of kids in grades 3 through 6, investigate how they are different from us when we were kids, and explore how to develop a writing environment that meets their needs.

In Part Two, Mentoring Tween Writers, I show how I serve as a mentor for students and demonstrate craft through personal writing. I also look at using mentor texts to build bridges between the reading and writing workshops.

Part Three, Sanity in a Test-Crazed World, is about testing pressures and balanced teaching. It's about the role of conventions in writing instruction—how to balance the need for proper conventions of print, the content of student writing, and achievement. Teaching conventions of print is a small part of writing instruction, but vital to communicating with the reader. I also show how to mix student-selected writing with required writing in many genres in order to prepare students for a variety of writing tasks.

The process of looking for answers to questions like these stimulates me. I love the challenge of examining my practices, love the flush that comes when my students succeed because I have become a better teacher.

If you're reading this book, you're a teacher who is searching too (that, or you need recertification credit). We need to delve deeper into these pressing questions, internalize the research available, and integrate this with our understanding of kids. We do this because this is our reward, our legacy, our mark on the world.

Even as I write these words, I am struck by how corny this sounds, how overly dramatic. I'm also struck by the truth of the statement. We thrive on learning; after all, the excitement of learning drew us to this profession in the first place.

To teach in this day and age is a daunting proposition. We're outnumbered and outgunned; we have little public support; we feel overwhelmed and undervalued. Yet we still love our jobs. We want something more from ourselves as learners; we want more for our students.

The more I read professionally, the more I know there are thousands of ways to teach writing well. I believe it is mature teaching to place the student at the center of the day, of the classroom. The security and predictability of the classroom and the sameness of the structure encourage risk taking.

Most important, though, I want my writing workshop to make a difference in the lives of my students. I want to use writing as a vehicle to get to know them better as human beings and to be part of their lives.

This book isn't about picture-perfect classrooms or picture-perfect rosy-cheeked kids skipping into classrooms, brains brimming with glorious prose. It's about real classrooms, real problems, real solutions, real teachers . . . and real kids who write. It's messy, sometimes uncomfortable, sometimes nerve-wracking. But it's always real.

I just thought you should know up front. I just thought that would be fair.

1

Understanding Tween Writers

It's not easy being a preteen. A lot of us are either in a tunnel or on a bridge. A lot of us don't know who we are. Instead of following Barney's advice, we end up doing what popstars do.

Kelley, age 10

As I get older, people give up on magic, stop believing in heaven . . . as I get older, I wish I would get younger.

Eric, age 12

They were easily the brightest *and most challenging* collection of kids I had ever had. These fifth graders were all shapes, all sizes, and every extreme— independent, strong-willed, tough, loving, and sensitive—and many of them held a general disdain for authority.

One morning, after a whole-class lecture about their outrageous behavior, I pulled kids back to the corner for individual "Come to Jesus" meetings. Luther Vandross's song, *The Power of Love*, played in the background to remind me that I actually loved them. After I let each kid have it, I rewound the tape and played it again. "Stay positive, stay positive," I told myself time after time as kid after kid shuffled back to meet me.

Next on my list was Sarah, a scrapper on the playground, a girl the boys feared, and first pick for every football game. She steadfastly refused to admit she was a girl and played football every recess. In kindergarten, when asked to line up as boys and girls, she had stood firmly in the boys' line. Yet this tough girl would sit docilely with her arm around me during every reading conference. That morning when I called Sarah's name, she knew she was in trouble. She sat down, and I launched into my speech. She interrupted, demanding, "Oh no, Mr. Morgan, don't even start on me, not until you rewind that tape!" I howled with laughter, rewound the tape, and then began my speech again. Tweens—at the very worst, they're honest.

Our classroom was quite the menagerie. Twenty-nine fifth graders, one harried teacher, two fish tanks, a litter-box-trained rabbit named Magic, and our evil, hateful gerbil, Spud.

Spud was a good match for that room. He was nicknamed "Fang" because there was nobody in the room he hadn't bitten. When kids yelled after being bitten, you could count on hearing a low "Another One Bites the Dust" chant from the corners of the room.

Early in the year, in a futile effort to stop the flow of blood from her finger, a student had allowed Spud to drop to the floor. He wouldn't use his leg for the rest of the day so Jenny, whose mom was a vet, took him home that night on the bus. After that, watching him run around with his tiny leg cast was enough to make even me feel a tinge of sympathy for him.

One morning as we lined up to go to gym, Jenny screamed out, "SPUD IS DEAD!" I began to curse under my breath. It was, of course, a school testing day. Timing. It figured. He was a pain in the rear alive, and he would be just as much of a pain in his death.

"Yep, he's dead," Whit laughed. The girls turned on him.

"Whit, shut up, you jerk!" Students began to cry. I was bewildered.

"We're late for gym. I'll check him out when you're gone," I assured them. As we walked down the hall, there was audible sobbing from many of the kids. I couldn't believe it. Why were they upset over that hateful rodent?

Our gym teacher, Kelly, looked at the crying faces, rolled his eyes, and brought the kids into the gym and without asking any questions began class. I went back to the classroom and nudged Spud fearfully, expecting him to rise and clamp down on my finger. He was dead all right. I found a small box to put him in.

Back in our classroom, I gathered the kids in our meeting area, figuring I should allow them time to talk about their grief. Tearful accounts of what Spud meant to them were shared. Tissues were passed around the circle. Then, in a move I would regret, I asked the class if they wanted to talk to Spud privately before he was buried. Kid after kid passed him around, whispering to him, and thus closing out a chapter. As Mark touched his fur, he jerked, almost dropped the box, and shouted, "He's alive! Spud's alive! He just moved!"

I cursed a bit more as I tried to regain order as kids fought to see. Spud moved again. Suddenly, Mike turned to me and announced coldly, "You . . . you . . . you almost buried him alive!" Suddenly, every eye in the room was on me, and they weren't loving, admiring glances!

"But I . . ."

For the rest of the morning, we posted "ICU nurses" by Spud's cage to keep us advised of his progress. Like town criers, students shared news of his condition as they changed shifts. Their interactions with me were icy at best. Spud's return to life was short-lived, though, and by lunchtime even the "nurses" admitted that he was truly, officially dead.

I retrieved the box from the desk, put Spud in it, and borrowed a trowel from the janitor. During lunch, I watched my kids on the playground from the door, wanting to give them some space. After lunch, they cradled the box as they walked to a private, isolated spot in a corner of the playground. The February wind tore at their coats and tangled their hair as they dug at the frozen soil, but it didn't seem to matter. After Spud was reverently committed to the earth, they stood in a circle around his grave for the remainder of the recess, crying and talking.

As they came back in the room, I hugged them, sad for their loss and emotional that I didn't feel more. We gathered again to talk. "I loved him *because* he was so mean," D. T. announced. "He always acted the way I feel."

"You know, that gerbil could get away with anything. It was like he could do what he wanted to, like he didn't even have to say to himself that he shouldn't because he was just going to do it anyway," Sarah blubbered, as kids around her scrambled to get her the Kleenex box. The tough veneer was gone, revealing her gentleness.

The passing of a gerbil was duly marked that day. These kids felt their loss fiercely. It was one of those moments, too few, too precious. I knew it was a brief break. Tomorrow would be different. But in one of a thousand moments that year, those kids wormed their way into my heart. They felt fiercely what their heart told them to feel. That week, we wrote about Spud.

Tweenhood

We need to know whom we're teaching and how tweens are different from other age groups if we are to be effective. Many teachers avoid this age group because these kids are so raw, so blunt, so cruel, yet so warm. When you tell people you teach intermediate kids, you rarely hear, "How cute. Isn't that a wonderful age?" More often than not you usually hear sighs of sympathy and responses like, "I could *never* teach that age group. You poor thing!" Some days I agree! Tweens, children between the ages of eight and twelve, are now being studied more by sociologists, educators, and even marketers. Ann Hulbert writes about how complex the age group can be to understand:

> For more than a decade now, it hasn't been just savvy marketers who have trained their sights on "tweens" . . . This stage, experts warn, is when children are either launched—educationally, socially, and emotionally—or get lost and left behind. Yet here, amid the stirrings of sexuality and the pressures of group conformity, is where parents first have to contend with peers as they try to retain any influence. So do teachers: Calls for more self-directed, "hands-on" learning in the "academic wasteland" alternate with exasperated sighs about terminally distracted students.
> Ann Hulbert (2003)

We were surprised that third graders were included in this tween phenomenon. They just seem so much younger and more innocent . . . at least until March when the horns start to sprout. When the decision was made to include our third-grade team with the intermediate grades instead of the primary planning teams, the third-grade teachers were relieved. They knew their kids didn't fit with the K–2 kids.

Researchers may be busy trying to define what a tween is, but teachers of eight- to twelve-year-olds know it in our hearts because we live with them every day. One of my teammates, Deb, captured it when she wrote,

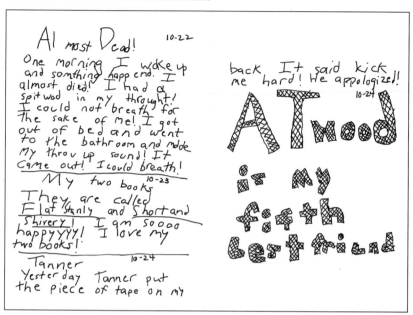

Tweeners. In between. Not yet teenagers, no longer little children. They're starting to see themselves as autonomous entities, separate from their parents, yet they struggle to figure out where they fit. They're proud because they have been deemed old enough to sit at the grown-up's table, yet secretly long to be back with the little kids, giggling and throwing peas. They happily play with Bratz dolls with a younger sister one day and pore through teen magazines and experiment with makeup the next. They view members of the opposite sex as probable carriers of cooties, while passing notes about kissing (or much more!) on the playground.

We found two pages that third-grader Brad wrote in his Living Book (our version of a writing journal) toward the end of the year. They mark many of the themes that are important to tweens (see Figure 1.1). Brad is both fascinated and alarmed by body functions. He is easily hurt by his peers and keeps track of who his friends are. And yes, reading and writing are part of the picture, too.

During this period, tweens need teachers around them who know that deep inside they are loving and warm, that under the sarcasm quality human beings are emerging. We need to identify the tenderness, the loving acts, so we can temper the verbal slams and body actions that force us to use our parents' phrases like, "Don't make me come over there!" They will let us into their lives if we are able to laugh at their comedic routines and situations.

Over the past two years, my colleagues and I have asked our students in grades 3 through 6 what it is like to be a tween today. We all knew our own childhoods were vastly different from the lives our kids lead. I grew up in a small town in Ohio, a town where high culture was viewing the county fair tractor pull from the top of the bleachers. Hi-tech was "rabbit ears" with the optional aluminum foil on the tips to better pull in the three Columbus TV stations on a black-and-white television.

The only terrorist I knew was Clyde Caulkins, a fifth grader who was old enough to drive to school . . . a slicked-back, greased-hair, woolly mammoth who smoked cigarettes outside the school grounds and daily relieved every kid of any spare change he or she was foolish enough to carry. Terrifying for me, yet nothing compared to life since 9/11, which is the world our tweens inhabit.

When we asked students what it was like to be a tween, did we ever get an earful. We were stunned by their comments, by the challenges they face, and by their grace in handling their situations.

As we opened the discussion in Deb's room, one young man told us about his GI Joe. It had always been more than a toy; it was more play-mate, conversation partner, and secret friend than doll. He talked about the first time a trusted friend made fun of him for still having it. After his buddy left, he sat and cried. Then in a fit of manliness, he decided to put the doll in his closet.

But he couldn't let GI Joe go entirely.

So, he put GI Joe on a shelf in the closet where he could still see it. Every week, he moved GI Joe farther and farther back into the dark, away from the door, until he didn't miss it so much.

Sometimes we minimize what kids are going through, especially as they become more sensitive to relationships with family and friends. Kimberley expresses this well:

> Sometimes my mom thinks I'm getting upset over everything. She says it's part of growing up, that might be one reason, but sometimes every-thing gives me a good reason to be upset.
>
> It's hard being this age because everyone starts to get very judge-mental and they let the impresions stick forver.
>
> Kimberley

P.S. Mr. Morgan, pease don't tell anyone that I wrote this. Make up some name like Amanda and tell people she doesn't want her identity shared.

The judgment of peers is arbitrary, brutal, and a constant source of concern for kids as they move through the upper elementary grades, as Dylan succinctly states:

When I was younger, everyone liked the same thing. But now, not now, now if you don't, you are out. I mean it. Out.
    Dylan

Marina, a fourth grader, describes the conflict of growing up but not wanting to be a teenager and wanting her sister to stay young:

I am starting to realize that I am old enugh to do anything. I now I am old enugh that I don't want to be a teenajeor.
    Just like if you have an older sister and say she likes a lot of boys just remind her that she can hang with you gis and just reminder how to be a kid. I am alwas trying to tell my sister that she can still be a kid.
    She is tring to be a grownup but I am down hear tring to pol her down to earth and its like she is poling one way I am poling the other way. She is going higher, I am going deeper. Just as I should.
    Marina

In our school district, sixth graders are still in elementary schools. Watching our third graders and sixth graders on the playground, listening to them in class, and reading their writing give me constant evidence of how rapidly and radically tweens change. One moment they're innocents, the next moment they are young adults.

Students in Deb's sixth-grade class were engaged in a team competition to earn points based on good work habits. Coming back from lunch one day, Jason impatiently said to his teammates, "Come on guys, settle down. We want to score!" There was a moment of silence. Then Ted, Rick, and Chris started punching each other and chortling, "Yeah, we want to *score!*" Their understanding of the sexual connotation was clear. They could easily have been sixteen or seventeen years old.

Many tweens show a keen awareness of family dynamics and of their own ambivalence about getting older. In fourth-grader Makenzie's writing, you can hear her mother's voice at the start of the piece. Then in her own voice, she distances herself from her mother as she imagines a day when she will have more choice of how and where and with whom she spends her time.

> *I'm starting to realize that "Don't waste life, stop playing video games" is good. Playing video games all the time is a waste of time you need to turn off the TV and get outside for goodness sake. Video games make the brain go into circles.*
>
> *So have a blast in life just have a blast and get outside!!!!!*
>
> *I want to be a teenager because you have fun and have more friends and you look cute too and you get to go to the mall with your friends. And you get your freedom to.*
>
> Makenzie

Tweens experience a great deal of conflict about growing up. They want to grow up, but at the same time, they don't want to leave childhood behind. For example, last week, one of my fourth graders came in the room, clearly upset. When the room was settled and busy, I pulled Parker aside and asked him what was on his mind.

"Parker, what's up? You look really sad."

He looked at me intently and declared, "Did you know there is no tooth fairy?" I nodded my head. "My parents kept it a secret from me. They hadn't told me when I was ready. I was ready when I was eight. I really want to know now. If they weren't honest about that, what else don't I know?"

"Is this really a situation about honesty, Parker? The tooth fairy is a common symbol of growing up."

"I had a clue in second grade that my parents had done that because I had a girl, Rena, in second grade and she told me in second grade. I believed it a little, but when I asked my parents, they told me there was one, so I believed them that there really was a tooth fairy. They should have told me. I was ready when I was eight."

"Parker, why do you think we have the story about the tooth fairy?"

"I don't know. It isn't fair. One time when I lost my first tooth [pointing] it hurt really bad, really bad when it came out."

"And what happened?"

"It finally came out, and it was bloody and gross, and I did what my parents told me, and put it under the pillow even though it was gross. I got a quarter for it!" he related smiling.

"So, it was painful and then you had this cool thing happen and got a quarter for it. So, why do we have the story about the tooth fairy?"

"Ohhhhhhh, I get it."

"Your parents want you to enjoy the phases of life, and we have customs that help us through those phases and let us believe in things. It's kinda like the Easter Bunny. . ."

"Now, I *know* the Easter Bunny is real. I check on that one every Easter when we go to Safeway and my parents *never* buy that candy."

I began to sweat. I had almost blown the cover. Thank goodness I hadn't brought up Santa Claus!

Sometimes I get duped into thinking that everything is serious for our kids today, that they're overburdened and harried. That is as much a mistake as assuming their lives are easy. One day the group of sixth-grade boys who had wanted to *score* were totally engrossed in the classic movie *Lassie Come Home*, (in which Elizabeth Taylor was a tween). They jeered at the trainer who mistreated Lassie, cheered for Lassie when she made her escape, gasped when Lassie's torn feet left bloody prints, urged Lassie on as she struggled the last few miles toward home, and applauded when Lassie and the boy she loved were finally reunited. They could easily have been six years old.

When I read something written by Jake, one of our sixth graders, I howled with laughter that he would admit to being such a kid:

> *When I was a young kid all I would do was run around in my boxers*
> *watching Scooby Doo claiming that I saw every episode. Now as a*
> *Tyweener I can't remember any of them at all.*
> Jake

It's always such a pleasant surprise to realize they're not as worldly as they sometimes seem, to see the parts of them that are still in childhood. I stopped breathing until I realized what Eddie really meant when he described his life as a twelve-year-old:

> *My mom is neglecting sex so it makes me feel weird. I already know*
> *about it but she still won't let me see movies with it in it. It's not like I*
> *want to but she acts like it's a disease. She's very pertective of me.*
>
> *I'm sure it's hard for my parents having a tween around the house.*
> *I'm messy and careless.*
> Eddie

And then, there's Hudson. After talking about what it means to be a tween all morning as a class, after writing about it for an hour, after discussing it for thirty minutes, he blurted out, "I don't get what all this deal is about. What is it about, all this Twinkie stuff? Like, get over it."

Tweens, Learning, and Self-Esteem

Tweens can't be stereotyped. Each kid is unique, so different from other kids in the class, and sometimes even different from who he or she was yesterday.

Although it is not a teacher's place to feel sorry for kids, sometimes I can be so inclined because of the horrifying conditions some face daily. I want to sympathize with them and talk about their situations with them, while pushing them to be great people and learners. But our job is to create a safe classroom, a place where, because kids are safe and loved, they can take risks, push boundaries, and become scholars.

Sometimes, when I have had it with the surly comments, the one-liners, the gotta-have-the-last-word syndrome and I think I want to work with younger kids, my colleague Dawn passionately points out, "If not us, who will teach this age kid? If it's going to be us, we have to understand these kids—what they think, how they feel—so that we don't misread their actions."

We have done the job if our students are proud that they are smart and happy that they are learning. What a joy to see kids happy and smiling because they pushed past their limits and became more literate; because they can produce incredible writing, see different points of view, think on their own, read, and apply that learning to new situations.

It's what we're here to do as teachers. Period.

2

Writers' Workshop

In all the professional books about teaching writing, there's the all-important scene between teacher and student when they determine the fate of the writing piece in front of them. It's a dramatic moment, charged with energy and the promise of an adolescent best seller.

> **Teacher** (*pencil tucked behind her ear, looking earnestly at the student, talking in a reverent, hushed tone*): What would you like to do with this piece?
>
> **Student** (*happily*): Oh, I want to publish it!
>
> **Teacher** (*beaming*): Great idea. When would you like to have this published?
>
> **Student** (*a faint smile spreads across her face, revealing dimples*): Oh, by early next week.
>
> **Teacher** (*bursting with pride*): That would be wonderful! We'll look forward to the debut.

The student rises and returns eagerly to her seat, the Enya music playing in the background rises in a crescendo, and the teacher wipes a tear from her eye. The student sits and excitedly begins to write with single-minded passion. The remainder of the classroom is on task and engaged in different stages of the writing process.

Yeah, right!

Over the course of twenty-four years of teaching, this conversation has never happened . . . not once. Ever! Noticeably absent in this scenario are kids crawling under desks, kids giggling and whispering about who's going out with whom, kids wandering around distracting all the other writers in the classroom, kids working very hard at not working.

Many things sound great in the professional books about writing that absolutely, positively do not work the same way for me. Maybe it's me; maybe it's the way I present the information. Recently, flush with excitement about turning over control of print conventions to the kids, I introduced a plan for student inquiry into various punctuation marks, hoping if they owned the work, they'd internalize the learning. The book I read portrayed this as an idyllic moment. As I laid out the plans with the kids, Tanner blurted out, "Oh Gawd! Don't tell me you want us to do that! I liked it better when you fixed everything!"

I have finally found what works for me when it comes to writing workshop structure and practice. And it doesn't always look like the classrooms in other books.

Scheduling Writing

One of the biggest challenges is putting all the pieces of the writing program together in a way that flows and is cohesive. This is a huge challenge. After some trials and errors, I've divided the writing block into the following segments:

8:20–8:30	Come in, hang up coats, sharpen pencils, talk with friends, etc.
8:30–8:45	Living Books
8:45–9:00	Whole-class crafting lesson
9:00–9:50	Composing and invitational groups
9:50–10:00	Reflecting and response
10:00–10:15	Spelling demonstration and practice

This structure has some leeway so that on some days we spend a few more minutes on one activity and less time on another.

Of course, your circumstances will determine how much time you spend on each element of the writing block. It's best when you can assemble uninterrupted time blocks, but it isn't always possible. Therefore, spelling might have to be fit into another time slot later in the day, or the student reflection time might occur while killing the ten minutes between lunch recess and specials. Some juggling is required to make the schedule work, but the rewards are well worth it.

Many people, when visiting a writing workshop, leave with the impression that the room is unstructured. Nothing could be further from the truth. If anything, reading/writing workshop classrooms need to be more structured with routine procedures in place. In a good writing workshop, the structures may not be immediately visible because the teacher's role is less obvious than in other learning situations. Much of the teacher's usual role is taken over by students.

Living Books (15–20 minutes)

While the teacher is getting the classroom going (taking attendance and lunch count, etc.), the students are writing in their Living Books, a written record of their lives. This starts the day with students writing, gets them warmed up, and sets the tone for the day. Notebooks in hand, the entire class gathers on the carpet in a circle. This writing exercise encourages free writing and experimentation without fear of assessment and evaluation. (See Chapter 4 for more about Living Books and their use.)

Crafting Lesson (10–15 minutes)

This whole-class lesson determines the writing focus for the day. During this time the teacher demonstrates in front of the entire class an effective writing technique or writing convention that we will work on that day or that week. This is the time to create a community of learners, to get them comfortable and excited about the task at hand, and to pose a challenge they will work on in their own writing.

This lesson sets the tone for the writing block and puts kids at ease to take on new learning challenges. This is the time to present the lessons I want every student to hear. The demonstrations are focused on observations from students' writing, such as a common concern or an area that is presenting a particular challenge. The demonstration can also show a new technique to expand their options as *writers*.

I draw many ideas for crafting lessons from the work of Ellin Keene and Susan Zimmerman (1997), who have categorized the types of lessons that are most effective. (See Figure 2.1.) They give many examples of crafting lessons in Chapters 6 and 7 of their book *Mosaic of Thought*.

Composing and Invitational Groups (30–60 minutes)

During this time students write on their own, seeking to approximate the techniques demonstrated during the crafting lesson. They are focusing on the lesson just presented, as well as on their personal goals as writers that I have identified.

This is also a good time to set up invitational groups, to invite students with like needs to gather for help. I may bring together several kids to work on an issue as basic as using capital letters for proper nouns or as difficult as using character development to convey an intended message to the audience.

During composing time, I circulate around the room, informally assessing who is getting the concept and who is not. It's a chance to see if the concept demonstrated in the crafting lesson took hold, took root. I carry a class list, quickly noting where kids are, and then use the results to determine the next teaching points in crafting lessons or to pull the invitational groups.

This is a busy time. I feel like the circus performer with the spinning plates on the sticks! Even though it can feel like there's too much to do and not enough teacher to go around, it can be a very productive time.

Reflection and Response (10–15 minutes)

All the students gather on the carpet to process the learning that occurred during the writing block. I ask kids who were successful to share how they used the concepts from the crafting lesson in their writing. I pose questions to the kids about the lessons of the day. They may share how they revised their lead to grab the audience or how they used quotation marks for a new speaker.

This time allows students to talk more about the techniques demonstrated earlier and to share how well they could put them into practice.

FIGURE 2.1 CATEGORIES FOR CRAFTING LESSONS

Fiction/Narrative/Expository/Memoir/Prose

Narrative Elements

Character
Static and dynamic
Methods for introducing character—
  exposition, action, dialogue

Setting
Time—flashbacks, fast-forward,
  manipulation of time through
  variations in conventions, sentence
  structures, word choice

Narration
First person (present and past)
Third person (limited or full
  omniscience, present or past)
Inanimate (objects narrate the piece)

Conflict
Internal or external
Person vs. person, person vs. nature,
  person vs. himself

Sequence of Events
Leads and endings
Rising action and denouement
Climax
Circular plots
Parallel plots
Foreshadowing

Stance
Efferent or aesthetic
Sympathetic or antagonistic
Global or focal

Text Structure

Conventions
Manipulation of punctuation for
  particular purposes

Word Level
Use of powerful nouns and verbs
  rather than excessive use of
  adjectives and adverbs in descriptive
  writing
Repetition of words to achieve effects
  that align with content
Word choice and usage to achieve
  effects that align with content

Sentence Level
Length and variety of sentences and
  manipulation of both to align with
  content
Repetitive sentence patterns to achieve
  an effect aligned with content

Text Level
Skillfully using beginning, middle, and
  end
Drafting compelling leads and endings
Manipulating pacing of plot
Voice-writing in a way that permits the
  reader to "hear" the writer's voice
  and his or her individuality as a
  writer
Writing to particular audiences and for
  particular purposes

Topic Choice

Mining a writer's notebook for topics
Observing the world for topics
Taking inspiration from mentor texts
Following your passions
Using shared experiences
Using prompts (no more than 20
  percent to 30 percent of the time)

They might discuss places where they stumbled, recognize their progress, or connect one lesson to another. It can help to solidify the new learning. This reflection ends the writing block.

Spelling (15 minutes)

Spelling issues are explored both in isolation and in the context of writing. (See Chapter 9 for details.)

Basic Workshop Elements

Debbie Miller, a valued colleague and author of the book *Reading with Meaning* (2002), has helped me to organize my thoughts about what needs to be in place for a classroom to run itself as much as possible. Miller's categories summarize the necessities for an effective writing classroom:

* Community
* Environment
* Time
* Rituals and procedures
* Gradual release
* Choice
* Response

Woven in and out of these categories are Brian Cambourne's conditions for learning (1993). Cambourne states that certain conditions will increase student engagement in learning and provide them more success. He believes that students' engagement in the learning will increase if they are

* *immersed* in the concept and text,
* given ample *demonstrations* of the lesson,
* surrounded by trusted adults who hold *high expectations* for their learning and support their growth,
* expected to make decisions about how and when they learn the concepts and given *responsibility* for the learning,
* provided ample *time* to use and practice the concepts,
* given the luxury of *approximation* and expected to make mistakes as they grab hold of the concept, and
* offered *feedback or response* from more knowledgeable classmates or teachers.

Students are more likely to try the concepts being taught when they are in a safe environment. When I can free them from external distractions and quiet the overriding insecurities of tweenhood, they can concentrate their energies on the tasks at hand.

Community

The feeling of community comes from knowing that you're part of something bigger than you. It's the safety net for the classroom, the setting that allows all of us in the room to take risks. Without a sense of community, a shared sense of place, the classroom will not gel. Creation of community flows directly from the teacher's behavior and attitudes, which model the desired types of interactions. Community grows as students copy their teacher's behavior and adopt their teacher's attitudes.

Community is built on unambiguous standards for behavior. I insist on a civil, polite space in which to gather. I acknowledge and reward, with verbal compliments and physical touch, respectful behavior. A pat on the back reinforces the connection between us. When disciplining kids and insisting on changes, I strive to acknowledge their need to save face and treat them with respect so they can maintain their dignity.

The tone of the room is set when the importance of each individual is validated. Every student in the room should know that he or she is valued and worthwhile, regardless of any reputation or previous encounters. It's as simple as letting students know you miss them when they are absent . . . even if it's that one kid that you secretly wished had come down with pneumonia!

Our community changes as students move in and move out. Our citizens are so mobile that many kids attend numerous schools, even in the course of one year. We want them to know that if they move away, we will never be the same again, that we will remember them. References to and remembrances of kids well after they have moved reinforce that each kid is important. We take time on a student's last day to verbalize how they have affected our lives. We try to keep touch via e-mails sent during writing time.

Community can be enhanced by sharing your own life in your writing, modeling writing techniques, and letting students get to know you as a person (within appropriate boundaries, of course). It is strengthened by recording classroom activities in written form, by celebrating our achievements and triumphs, and by dealing honestly with our sorrows and troubling or difficult life events.

The classroom needs to be safe, under control, predictable, and secure, and somebody must clearly be in charge. Class meetings where students are free to raise concerns about whatever is affecting them at the moment can provide an outlet for issues to be aired and resolved.

A good sense of community

* is directly related to teacher modeling of behaviors.
* sets the tone for the room.
* is built on standards of behavior.
* provides a safe environment for risk taking.
* is fluid but stable as people move in and out of it.
* is a responsibility shared by teacher and students.
* occurs when students know they are loved, valued, and essential to the classroom.
* celebrates the events we share in our lives.

Environment

Environment is all about making the space clean, inviting, and warm. I like a lived-in room, a place that looks like a Pier One Imports shop. I've had to pare down since our school switched to a year-round schedule; every nine weeks, I have to take down the entire room, pack it up, and move out; then when I return after break I have to move into and set up another room.

But I still stack it full of books, plants, magazines, and science experiments. A few Garfield posters slammed on a wall don't constitute ambiance for tweens. Environment changes attitudes and perspectives and gives students a sense of space. Tweens need a combination of open space that they can construct to suit themselves at any one time and enclosed space with borders that clearly indicate the physical limits of safety. They need both order and room to explore and experiment.

I have a very large group meeting area for whole-class crafting lessons. The flip chart, markers, and picture books are all right there. When possible, it's good to have a light there as well, to make this the focal point of the room.

Whoever is presenting at the time has a comfortable chair to sit in. There are lights all over the room so I don't have to use those hated fluorescent ones overhead. The warmer light sets a tone, a mood; it softens things and makes both teacher and kids more comfortable.

Books are displayed on rolling carts and in tubs in the library area. The categories are determined by the students and teacher so everyone knows the arrangement. Some books are in tubs by authors, some by subject, some by series, some by genre: all labeled and organized by kids. The kids help determine this and manage this system so they own it.

Students' desks are arranged in clusters so there's more meeting space. I try to provide some quiet areas for a respite from the busyness of the room, as well as areas for more noisy activity. I try to reinforce that if you choose to work at your desk, it means you need the quiet so the rest of us will respect that. Conferences and small group meetings take place in the common areas.

It's good for kids to care for living things. We have lots of plants in the room and in a large fish tank we have aquatic frogs that move and amuse. We still miss our classroom rabbit, guinea pigs, and other animals since the district's ban of fur-bearing animals. We are on the lookout for animals we can humanely have in the room.

I am a nut for a clean classroom. Every Friday, without fail, I have Roto-Rooter time. Desks are dumped, backpacks emptied and sorted, desktops washed, windows cleaned, paper restocked, boards washed, plants watered, fish tanks cleaned, papers passed out, notebooks weeded out and organized, lunch basket washed, pencil boxes sorted, and stray clothes returned to their owners. Students are assigned, as one of the class jobs, to monitor and inspect desks and backpacks so I can rove and manage the chaos.

This twenty-minute block produces a cleanliness and has a purpose. It adds a sense of order to the room and is a statement that we care about the room and work to maintain it. First impressions mean a lot, similar to the "curb appeal" of a house for sale.

I also think it helps kids who are rather cluttered in their thinking to clean out mentally and organize. It saves time finding things, and I can usually move desks without everything falling out.

An attractive, clean room also shows a way to live that is different from what some kids have experienced. Last year I drove home a student who had missed the bus. None of the phone numbers we had on file worked, and somehow her "daddy of the month" had missed the fact that his little girl wasn't home yet. From the doorway to her home, I counted seven piles of dog excrement on the carpet. I was astounded by the smell and filth and the mountains of dirty dishes piled in the sink. Some kids need to know there's a different way to live. And these kids aren't learning how to clean and organize at home either by osmosis or by instruction from parents.

I look at pathways for traffic flow to see if kids can easily get around the room. Materials for their use are in easy access and the kids know how to load the stapler, where to find sticky notes, and where to go when we run out of supplies. A student supply manager fills out the office requisition for more staples and paper clips and then I initial the request.

A healthy learning environment

* welcomes you in.
* is a clean, attractive place that is comfortable and user friendly.
* sets the tone for the classroom.
* shows that the room is well run and organized.
* seeks to turn control of the space over to the students.
* facilitates learning and provides different settings for changing moods and various personalities.

Our classroom environment invites people in and asks them to stay and spend some time. It's our living room.

Time

When stressed, I often try to cram too much into my plans. A stressed-out teacher gets agitated, which, in turn, creates snappy, irritable kids who lash out. I have to monitor this unhealthy cycle.

I believe in the "less is more" theory, even though I don't always practice it! Our school, our city, our culture seem to be in this frantic crisis mode. I eat breakfast in the car and read memos and notices while walking down the hall. It's ridiculous.

Cambourne (1993) talks of the need for time to "approximate" new learning. If learners are trying something new, they need uninterrupted time to experiment and to revise their work as they receive and process feedback from others in the room.

I can try to slow the world down a bit in our classrooms. Slowing the frantic pace and focusing on fewer things for longer bits of time is a worthy goal. For example, using the same picture books for reading and writing demonstrations frees some time to go into depth on one book instead of covering lots of different books. I integrate science and social studies content during reading to free up time.

Time

* can be managed so a measured pace facilitates learning.
* can be maximized for learning if fewer topics and concepts are dealt with in depth.
* can be exploited by searching for ways to integrate learning into several subject areas.

Procedures

Established classroom procedures allow me to teach effectively. As we start the year, the students and I chart procedures for everything we do, from going to the bathroom to sharpening pencils. Before we embark on anything, we review the procedures relating to that activity. For example, we read the chart posted above the hallway door about expectations before going to lunch. As we begin the writing block, we review expectations for use of time, procedures for setting up a conference, conference length, location of supplies, and what to do when you're finished with a piece of writing.

We never think of all the things that will require procedures before we start a new year, so the first couple of weeks, any time we see something that might become a management issue, I add it to a list of concerns to be brought up in a whole-class meeting. It's surprising what we forget. For example, instead of being shocked or going ballistic when a student gets up during read-aloud to throw away a snack wrapper, I add it to a list of procedures we need to revise.

Delegating as many responsibilities in the room as possible not only gives the kids responsibility for running the room, it also frees me to interact with kids and be available to them. I assign jobs every month or two because I want to give them time to get accustomed to the job. I also let them speak to the class when there are issues related to the performance of their respective jobs.

Examples of students' jobs and responsibilities are:

* Botanist: water and care for plants.
* Food-Service Manager: take lunch count, give attendance to teacher, bring lunch basket to the lunchroom.
* Supply Manager: stock writing cabinets and put sticky notes on teacher's desk when supplies are low.

*   Librarian: organize the library during Roto-Rooter time and talk to the class when there are issues.

The students' responsibilities include taking action when things are not running smoothly. When the class starts getting lax with caring for our library, the class librarians raise the issue with the rest of the class and ask for help. When kids are forgetting to check in for their lunch choice, the class food-service managers voice their frustration, and so on.

Students have a role and have a vested interest in classroom structures and procedures. Tweens love the responsibility of running the room, and I love to turn over control to them. Anything that takes me away from teaching (e.g., taking lunch count, stocking the writing supplies, keeping the schedule of who will share writing) can be turned over to the kids.

Taking the time to establish procedures at the beginning of the school year is important. Rushing through procedures and processes to get to the content will cost dearly because you have to spend bits of time here and there all year going over procedures. Moving on before procedures are internalized will require constantly reinforcing routines instead of teaching; both teachers and students suffer when instructional time is spent reinforcing procedures and putting out fires. And it tends to make us cranky.

It's important to be aware that some kids feel more comfortable running the room, *my life*, and the world and have little time to be a kid. One year, Tracey, who had to get her three younger brothers up, dressed, fed, and on the bus, was so involved in running the room that I had to put limits on her. I finally put her in charge of the school calendar on my desk, and that was all she was allowed to do.

Tracey would remind me of upcoming meetings, as well as add assemblies and appointments as the school announcements were made in the morning. As payment for her time that year, she received Scholastic Book Order vouchers. It was the only year I actually made it to all the school assemblies. Not once that year did I wonder why the school was so quiet, only to realize later that we had missed a Jump Rope for Heart assembly.

Procedures

*   keep a sense of predictability and order.
*   prevent wasting time on activities that don't contribute to learning.
*   contribute to a sense of community by delegating and sharing responsibilities.

    *   prevent small needless irritations and keep the atmosphere pleasant.

Rituals

Classroom rituals help the teacher manage the class and increase the students' comfort level so everyone can focus on learning. Keeping the daily schedule and procedures as stable and predictable as possible not only helps kids with transitions, but it also allows kids to plan their time.

In my class, each day begins the same way. I stand in the doorway greeting kids individually, checking in with them, getting a feel for how they are and what is going on in their lives. They prepare for the day and then gather in the "Oval Office," a place to meet and make high-level decisions.

While they wait for everyone to arrive, kids have time to get caught up with friends. It's a social time, when kids talk and enjoy one another's company. I get all the necessary daily paperwork finished, frame the day, and then begin the crafting lesson.

I end the day the same way. After cleanup, the students who are Building Inspectors dismiss table groups to the Oval Office, where we review the day and set expectations for the evening and the following day. It sounds serene, doesn't it? Wrong. I spend more time agonizing over the last ten minutes of the day than anything else. I really want to end the day calmly, but it's never as smooth as the start of the day.

We have another ritual called "The Days of Our Lives," where we select the most memorable or most humorous event of the day. A student volunteers to illustrate the event on a file card. For example, if the event is the first day of school, the chosen kid may draw a picture of a school bus and write the words, "First Day." These cards are glued onto butcher paper, in chronological order, and this strip of butcher paper is stapled way up on the wall by the ceiling to keep wall space for their writing and thinking. It's a visual documentation of our lives together.

I don't always get to this ritual daily, so I keep a list of notable events on the wall, and sometimes on a desperate Friday afternoon, I pass out the events accumulated on the list and the kids illustrate them.

Author celebrations are another ritual of our classroom. Usually, they happen after every publishing deadline and are attended by everyone who has made the deadline. Together we decide how to celebrate. Sometimes we have book-signing events where our authors sign copies of their work; sometimes we have Poetry Hour when our published poets give readings.

Some rituals exist to calm students and ease transitions. Immediately as the kids return from lunch or recess, they come to the Oval Office for read-aloud. It sets a nice tone and distracts them so they forget some of the playground conflicts they were dying to talk about; it saves time dealing with smaller conflicts that don't really need the teacher's attention.

Rituals

* help the class function amid predictable structures.
* celebrate class events and build community.
* provide stability.

Gradual Release

A recurring theme in this book is to turn the room over to students and give them as much control as possible, include them in decisions, and have them more engaged in room procedures.

Of course, when introducing a new thinking or writing strategy or a new convention of print, the teacher is in control. The kids need to see the concept modeled correctly and then have a chance to try it out before they take on the learning for themselves.

As some students verbally express the concept, others try out the concept in their writing, and then students who are correctly using the concept can do the demonstrations for other kids. This "gradual release of responsibility" model (see Figure 2.2) was developed by David Pearson and his colleagues (Pearson and Gallagher 1983).

Gradual release works for introducing any new concept in writing. For example, if the class has been studying how authors use punctuation to make their message clear, I model reading a text to look for examples of punctuation that help the reader understand the author's message. Then I show how to log those realizations about punctuation. Then students can be turned loose to begin their punctuation research in pairs. As I see pairs of researchers who are especially productive isolating different ways to use punctuation, I have them demonstrate what they've discovered and how they've documented their new learning. This way control of the process is gradually shifted from teacher to students.

Eventually, I identify individual students who are effectively employing the technique or skill we are working to master. I meet with them to plan a mini-lesson they will teach to the class. It's good for the students to

FIGURE 2.2 GRADUAL RELEASE OF RESPONSIBILITY MODEL

Planning Phase
Teacher identifies strategy to be taught.
Teacher explores strategy in his or her own writing.
Teacher collects text to use in instruction.

Early Phase
Teacher models use of strategy.
Teacher confers with students over early attempts at strategy.
Students experiment with strategy and share early attempts.

Middle Phase
Teacher continues to model strategy through think-alouds.
Class explores use of strategy in different genres.
Teacher begins to connect strategy with previously explored strategies.
Teacher convenes small invitational groups to meet particular needs involving
    strategy.
Students begin to use strategy in other genres.
Students begin to show evidence of using the strategy independently.
Students share how they are using the strategy more deeply.

Late Phase
Teacher models strategy in challenging texts with smaller groups.
Teacher models strategy through "cold reads" of new texts to show how the
    strategy works in first-time use.
Students assume responsibility for explaining their use of the strategy.
Students teach mini-lessons using the strategy.
Students show how they can use the strategy in composing increasingly difficult
    text.
(This version of Pearson's gradual release model was adapted from Keene and Zimmermann 1997)

hear the new concept in as many ways as possible and from as many perspectives as possible.

Gradual release of control

* allows the teacher to engage with kids more effectively because
  more students are proficient with essential components of the
  writing lab.
* provides demonstrations to immerse writers in new concepts
  before they approximate the learning.
* establishes a sense of ownership as students turn into teachers.
* provides a variety of voices for discussing new learning in kid-
  friendly talk.

Choice

If students have a choice in what they write about, they will be more engaged, more productive, and more vested in the end product.

We alternate between student-selected writing topics and teacher-assigned studies focused on a curricular topic. When the students select their own topics to write about, many times those topics come from their Living Books (see Chapter 4). Teacher-assigned topics are usually selected from within a specific genre.

After students finish a genre study and writing in that genre, a student-selected topic allows expression of students' interests and passions. This self-selected topic accommodates many of the writers in the room who ordinarily receive acknowledgment in a school setting. Many times, this validates the passions of students who normally wouldn't receive attention for what they know outside of class because their peers support them and make connections to their topic.

In their research on adolescent boys' literacy, Michael Smith and Jeff Wilhelm (2002) and Tom Newkirk (2002) discuss the need for schools to broaden the scope of what we accept as good reading and writing. Smith and Wilhelm's book, *"Reading Don't Fix No Chevy's"* (2002), challenges teachers to look at stereotypes of boys and to realize that boys need a sense of competence and control, which can come from reading and writing about topics they're passionate about. Newkirk, in his book *Misreading Masculinity*, expresses the need for schools to broaden the literacy spectrum to allow more kids into the academic arena. He pushes teachers to avoid being literate snobs, to provide a "bigger room" that allows in more students.

This research led me to rethink comics as a genre, to bring in more magazines about various topics that might spur writing, to model my own passions, and to broaden my perspective about what is acceptable student choice. I no longer try to look down on Goosebumps types of books and student writing that tries to emulate them. I used to enjoy reading Captain Underpants, but not accept when students wrote similar types of manuscripts.

Of course, the class will not subsist on a diet of Captain Underpants type of writing. It's good to alternate the self-selected topics with genre writing. When we honor students' passions and topical choices, they honor our need to broaden their reading and writing in a variety of genres.

Student choice

* increases motivation and engagement because students have ownership.

* broadens the literacy circle and creates more options for readers and writers.
* allows for personal passions and supports students who do not fit naturally into the academic structure of school.
* results in better quality work and a more productive classroom environment.

Response

I realize more and more how much learning occurs when kids have time to reflect on their learning or on the learning process. Brian Cambourne (1993) says learners must receive feedback from other more knowledgeable sources, feedback that doesn't threaten the learners and allows them to refine their thinking.

Many times the most effective response comes from other kids. If a writer is sharing how he is using a punctuation mark, another student might respond in a way that pushes the thinking even further. If students are effectively sharing their new learning, the result will be even deeper understanding of that new learning. But response works best when the teacher gradually releases responsibility for it to students, after making certain that the kids understand how to "effectively share their learning."

For example, before we begin peer-writing conferences, I pay attention to students who are engaged during teacher/student writing conferences. I look for a student who can identify his or her needs as a writer, who responds as we talk, or who gets excited about possibilities for writing.

Once writers who are engaged with the process are identified, all students assemble around us in the Oval Office. We sit together in front of the rest of the class and then have a writing conference, called a fishbowl conference. Later, during a debriefing of the conference, I jot down words, phrases, and behaviors that made it a good or bad conference. These observations are posted in the room. I continue doing this, pulling different kids each day until it's clear that more and more students are catching on to what amounts to helpful and effective response to another's writing; then I release more control to the students.

Once a critical mass of the class is effectively conducting good conferences with me and once they have observed numerous fishbowl conferences with different kids, they're ready for peer conferences. While they confer in pairs, I rove the room, listening for great questions, responses, and engagement and observing conference behaviors. When I run into a great conference, it's worthwhile to stop the room, gather the students around the pair, and have them continue the conference as the rest of the room watches and documents behaviors. Later, we debrief as a class.

Some questions to pose are:

* What made that a great conference?
* What was effective?
* What was not very effective?

The responses and discussion clarify the learning and bring it into focus. It's sometimes helpful to chart students' comments and post them on the wall for future reference.

Dedicating time to responding to writing

* allows students to refine and share thinking.
* provides opportunity to make connections to other students' thinking processes.
* summarizes and contains new thinking.

Bringing Essentials (Back) to Life

Any time things in a classroom begin to fall apart, it can almost always be traced to a breakdown in one of the essential elements of a writing workshop. It is crucial at the beginning of the year to teach processes and procedures and address these issues as they arise throughout the year. Establishing procedures is critical, and so is maintaining them.

One morning last January I was sitting with my friends in the teachers' lounge while my students were at recess, and I was in a foul mood. None of my colleagues had noticed the deep sighs that periodically emanated from me. Finally, Barb caught on and asked, "What is the matter with *you*?"

"I hate them."

"Hate who?"

"Hate my kids. The thought of going up those stairs and facing their writing is putting me over the edge."

"You don't hate them," Barb responded, sugar dripping sarcastically from her voice.

"Yes, he does," Dawn replied. "This is gonna be good."

"I'm sick of their writing. It's awful lately—boring, unoriginal—and they don't use conference suggestions. They're playing around so much I feel like a cop walking around keeping them on task. I'm sick of it."

Barb's laughter cut me short. "What's wrong with you? Weren't you just saying last week that it's rarely the kids that are the problem, that it's usually your practices, your systems? Remember? Management problems usually come from laxness in those systems?"

"Yeah, yeah, yeah, so what's your point?"

"Have you asked the kids what's going on, or is this one of those 'don't walk your talk' things?"

I was ready with a smart-aleck response then realized she was right. "No, I haven't," I replied. "Maybe I need to."

"Oh geez, it's time to go," I said, jumping up. "That doesn't mean I don't hate them," I called over my shoulder as I left, my friends hooting and hollering. I stopped and turned. "And I hate you all too."

Luckily, I mellowed and relaxed a little before the kids came back in from recess. As the kids filed into our room, they read me quickly, as they always do.

"Uh-oh," I heard them say to each other, "he's mad!"

"Join me up here, please."

"Yep, he's mad!" Yamileth called out.

"I'm not mad," I snapped.

"He's mad all right," Thomas verified.

Once they were assembled in our meeting area, I laid out what I was seeing and feeling. "I am frustrated with the writing. It seems like we have stalled after months of incredible growth. All I do is walk around like some kind of prison guard. You're not paying attention to our conferences, which feels like a total waste of my time. You're missing deadlines. And, to tell the truth, the writing is so boring I can hardly stand it. What's up?"

Logan's hand shot up, as it always does. I was relieved he would start out because he always got me laughing at his dry wit while nailing most issues on the head. "You're asking us, right?"

"Right, why?"

"Just wondering. . . Is this one of those 'ask us for the truth, we tell you, then you get all mad' type of deals ? I'm not going there!"

I assured them they were safe. Once free to talk, they let loose. My crimes were:

* I had worn them out with personal narrative. They didn't feel they had any more heart-wrenching experiences that could earn a tear or two.
* I wasn't doing my job. I wasn't modeling new techniques for them, wasn't sharing my own writing, wasn't involved enough.
* I hadn't provided new audiences. Kaylee was sick and tired of sharing with her classmates. She wanted a break, wanted out of the room once in a while, wanted new audiences.
* We weren't celebrating anymore. Ashley quoted the date of our last author reception, two months previous.
* There wasn't enough choice. I was in charge. I determined what we were doing next without asking them about what they were interested in studying.

I then asked what their part was in the problem. They were equally honest, citing:

* Playing around too much (they blamed cabin fever).
* Being more concerned with friends than with writing.
* Placing responsibility for managing the classroom on me. Jen admitted that they were being lazy, that they were waiting for me to take charge instead of having a joint responsibility to run the room.

This incident illustrates how important the essential elements in a writing classroom are and how quickly they can spin out of control. Things had been running smoothly, then suddenly everything was out of whack. It's easy to dupe yourself into believing that once the classroom is running smoothly, it'll continue that way and you can relax. That's when things always fall apart.

Then there are those years that seem to never end. Those years when regardless of how many times you reinforce procedures and routines, every day seems like the first day of the year. During those years, *those* years, you hang on, reinforce, reinforce again, and then reinforce some more. And you dream of June!

3

Planning and Strategy Instruction

riters write for readers. And good readers make good writers. So, teaching writing strategies must incorporate lessons about good reading strategies. Teaching them can be very complicated because of the complex mental gymnastics required to read and write. Teaching reading and writing strategies to tweens is challenging because in any group of tweens there are greatly varied levels of ability and accomplishment. Also, it's easy to get caught up in a fun or successful strategy and neglect to connect it to other strategies. So, in addition to understanding tweens, teachers must be very clear about what they are teaching and how.

That said, lack of detailed planning doesn't necessarily make an ineffective teacher. A couple of anecdotes:

***

Years ago I was busy teaching when the principal walked into the room. The principal was gruff and direct and didn't mince words. At district meetings he would loudly announce, "I wholeheartedly believe in shared decision making." After a dramatic pause, he would add, "I make the decisions and then share them."

I saw him come in and straightened up. He wandered around the room, looked at my desk, came over to me, put his hand on my shoulder, and said quietly, "Mr. Morgan, you're one hell of a teacher."

"Yeah . . . and?"

"Do me a favor."

"Sure," I replied.

"Do up another set of weekly lesson plans." I looked perplexed. "It's May," he continued, "Your lesson plan book still says Thanksgiving Break."

"Got it."

❋ ❋ ❋

One spring, Sheri Kangas, a former teammate, and I attended the high school graduation of one of our favorite groups of kids. After the ceremony, we waited outside to greet the new graduates. Kids ran up screaming, hugging us, and sharing memories with us. It was a highly emotional event because the bond was still so strong all these years later. Their reactions and stories made it clear that we had had a positive impact on their lives. Kid after kid shared memories of the two years we had spent together. Looking at them, we were full of pride, in awe of who they had become. Not one kid mentioned that we should have planned better. Nobody said, "Those were two great years, but couldn't you have used your plan book more?"

❋ ❋ ❋

Even though we all know we can teach without lessons plans, organized and realistic planning is a crucial frame for our best teaching. It's very easy to be immersed in the moments of teaching and forget to step back and check the overview of what we should be teaching. The more explicit the plans, the better the instruction. (And lessons plans are tangible evidence to those who require proof.)

This past year, teammates Dawn Harbert and I vowed to plan together, be more reflective, and stay consistent with writing workshops and strategy instruction. When we met to discuss the requirements, we decided the planning template had to:

* be immoveable so we wouldn't lose it while roving around the room.

* be visual so we could quickly glance at it for refreshers about teaching intentions.
* be a work in progress so that we could easily revise plans based on what we accomplished that day.
* provide a blank section so that when we realized there was a common issue or need, we could go immediately to those plans and make a note before we forgot.
* allow planning as we taught because more often than not, once school ends, life is a whirlwind of meetings, e-mails, gathering resources, talking with parents, planning school events, and so on. It would have no dates on it to spare us some of the pressure of schedules.

Command Central

We established Command Central, a bulletin board on one wall of the classroom. It is a list of all the planning that we can quickly go to, check the plan, add what we need to do next, jot down informal assessment notes about kids, and begin to organize the following day.

Command Central includes sheets for the following areas (see the appendix for actual sheets):

Brian Cambourne's Conditions of Learning
Writing Crafting Lessons (whole-class lessons based on assessment, observations, and students' need)
Writing Invitational Groups (skills groups based on writing needs)
Reading Crafting Lessons (whole-class reading lessons)
Reading Invitational Groups (small groups based on reading needs)
Reading Check-in sheets (strictly survival, to keep track of what book they're reading and how much progress has been made)
Ellin Keene's list of comprehension/thinking strategies and how those strategies look in reading and writing

We decide what lessons need to be taught to immerse the writers in the concepts we are studying. These are lessons all kids will need regardless of assessment so we can list them on the Writing Crafting sheet ahead of time. Then we fill out the sheet on Cambourne's conditions, detailing how to immerse the kids in the concepts and teaching. The demonstration strategy becomes the reading and writing crafting lesson(s) and is listed on those sheets. We also list specific crafting lessons to teach based on informal and formal writing assessments.

We add to the list as we observe common issues while teaching. For example, if the kids are struggling to blend dialogue into the text, we go immediately to the planning sheets and add to the list of crafting lessons they need. If four kids are struggling to use paragraphs or quotation marks, we can go to Command Central and add their names to a list of kids for invitational groups (skills groups) to work on those elements.

When time allows, we evaluate the crafting lessons and note in the Reflection column how they went, which helps determine next teaching steps.

After determining the curricular focus, going through the Conditions of Learning provides a scaffold for our lessons. It's good to state ahead of time what we expect from the writers so they know how they'll be judged. We figure out how to share the responsibility for the learning with the kids, build in ways to allow approximation, and accommodate response time.

Planning for Integrated Strategy Instruction

Ellin Keene and the folks at the Public Education and Business Coalition (PEBC), a Denver nonprofit organization dedicated to improving reading and writing instruction in public schools, created a list of comprehension strategies and indicated how those strategies look across the curriculum. The complete list of strategy connections in reading and writing is in the appendix. When Dawn and I started to plan ahead, we wanted to use those strategies to guide the planning for both reading and writing.

We simplified the strategies for our use. We also changed the format from vertical to horizontal so we could easily track the strategy across reading and writing. Posting these sheets in Command Central kept them handy for easy viewing while teaching and planning. Figure 3.1 shows three of the sheets we use to link three strategies in reading and writing.

Comprehension strategies, paired with skills work and word work, are the keys to creating better readers and writers. The schema a reader needs to understand is identifiable, which makes it a fairly easy element to work on to improve a piece of writing. It makes good reading and writing less of a mystery.

It is one thing for kids to use strategies in a group and a totally different thing to use them when writing or reading by themselves. It's a good

FIGURE 3-1: SAMPLE READING AND WRITING STRATEGY LINKS

Determine Importance

Reading

1. Focus on key themes and on important and unimportant ideas within those themes.
2. Determine importance at the word level, sentence level, and text level.
3. Use text features and structure.
4. Delete information that distracts from the main idea.
5. Prioritize what is most important for long-term memory and synthesis.

Writing

1. Focus writing on key themes and ideas and decide what to include or delete to make the purpose of the writing more obvious.
2. Determine which words and sentences should carry the most weight to convey your message.
3. Choose the best genre and structure to convey your message.
4. Delete information irrelevant to the larger purpose.
5. Emphasize some elements to help the reader's comprehension and memory.

Draw Inferences

Reading

1. Use schema (prior knowledge) to draw conclusions.
2. Make and confirm predictions using textual clues.
3. Combine schema and text to answer unanswered questions.
4. Interpret your reading to deepen the experience according to the purpose of the reading.

Writing

1. Decide what information to include that will encourage readers' inferences.
2. Decide what to state explicitly and what to leave to interpretation.
3. Provide information necessary for the reader to make intended inferences.
4. Give only enough details to allow inference, instead of giving everything away.

Schema

Reading

1. Spontaneously activate schema before, during, and after reading.
2. Take in new schema and add to previous schema.
3. Use personal connections to relate to the text more deeply and store for future reference.
4. Use schema of other texts to comprehend the author's style, genre, and text structure.

Writing

1. Write from your experience, whether writing fiction or nonfiction.
2. Make the needed information explicit to yourself and your audience.
3. Know when schema is inadequate and offer necessary background information.
4. Choose specific format or genre to aid the reader's schema.

idea to assess strategy use over a considerable period of time and to check for individual use of the strategy during writing and reading conferences.

A Sample of Integrated Strategy Instruction

It's important to teach the strategy in reading *and* in writing. To increase the engagement with each strategy, we decided to focus on teaching the strategy in both reading and writing demonstration lessons.

For example, I use *Wilfrid Gordon McDonald Partridge* (Fox 1985) to teach schema connections in both reading and writing. It's a story about a young boy who lives next to a nursing home, and one of his favorite people there has lost her memory. The boy asks people in the home what a memory is, and then he brings objects from home to stimulate his friend's memory. Her memory returns as she beautifully and eloquently relates her experiences prompted by the objects the boy has brought to her.

As I read aloud to the kids, I reflect on my connections to older people losing their memory. On chart paper I write about my grandmother and my memories of her and her Alzheimer's disease. For example, I jot down the time grandmother disappeared while visiting our house one day, and the entire family desperately fanned out through the neighborhood to find her. I remember another time she wandered away, and the frantic search that ended when we found her, purse clasped on her lap, primly dressed in hat and coat, sitting in the Chevy with the windows rolled up in the 90-degree day. I write down the cryptic words she uttered as we opened the car door, "I'd be eternally grateful if you'd just take me home."

During this read-aloud, I also talk and write. And the kids chime in with stories about their grandmothers.

After we have studied how authors create necessary schema, we look at our own writing. We spend time talking about the schema our readers need to know before they write. Many times young writers need to explain things as they read their pieces aloud. For example, while reading her writing, a student might look up and say, "Now, this is my grandmother who lives in Arizona. She is really fun and cool. She brings me cool stuff. Sometimes I get to go there on vacation, and they have a pool in their backyard, and she swims with us and plays with us. She has these days when I get to do everything I want with just her. "

This is the time to jump in and say, "That schema should be in your writing. That is the schema that will let the reader know why you're so excited she is coming to visit."

Planning and Spontaneity

Does this sound overwhelming to you? It does to me. There's too much to do and too little time to do it! Good planning is essential. But good planning requires a realistic and reasonable approach. When thinking about planning, try to remember the following:

Planning models and templates must reflect teaching style.

The purpose of planning is to be more explicit with teaching moments and more consistent with instruction.

Less is more. Period. Spending more time on fewer topics reduces stress and aids internalization of the strategy.

Planning templates should allow for spontaneous teaching moments to provide best for students' needs, which are never completely predictable.

Planning templates should free the teacher to teach, not create unnecessary work and burden.

When planning, the more information at our fingertips, the more effective the planning; so keep favorite professional books and resources nearby.

Remember, we have these kids for only one year; they are in school for thirteen years. We cannot do it all. It's a team effort.

It's very difficult to be consistent in planning, to keep the day flowing instead of getting chopped up. The planning is the framework that sets the stage for all learning. It gives both teachers and tweens the structure and pacing to get it all done, or most of it anyway. By planning as we go, we can avoid those "Thanksgiving Break" fiascos!

Living Books

The biggest frustration with writing workshop is probably topic selection. When it was time for some students to start a new writing topic, I cringed inside waiting for the inevitable, "I don't know what to write about." Patiently and calmly, I pulled the kids struggling with new topic selection into a small group and went through painstaking brainstorming. Typical exchanges went like this:

> **Teacher:** What was your favorite vacation?
> **Student:** (*blank stare*)
> **Teacher:** What was your most memorable experience? What is a story you tell over and over again that you need to get on paper?
> **Student:** (*blank stare*)

With each blank stare, frustration mounted. Finally,

> **Teacher** (*voice raised in frustration*): Why don't you write about the football game where you made your first touchdown?

Student: Oh, I didn't think about that.

In such an exchange, as if following a script, I would get very agitated and deliver the following speech:

> *Why do I know more about all your lives than you do yourself? Why do I know what you should write about next and you* don't? *Who is living your life anyway? There are twenty-seven of you and I know more about you than you know of yourself!*

The speech became as much a part of my classroom procedure as the writing itself. It was my version of dad yelling up the stairs, "Don't make me come up there!" Predictable, consistent, routine. Just like the professional books recommend about running the writing workshop. Keep it predictable, consistent, and routine.

The kids, perhaps laughing, perhaps shamed, would look at me and shuffle back to their desks to begin doodling on their papers.

Clearly, this was not the best way to teach. I had to do something, but didn't know what until I stumbled on Joanne Hindley's book, *In the Company of Children* (1996). Her writing program includes writers' notebooks, notebooks the kids write in every day. Voilà! The answer to the problem of topic selection.

Because it is a record of life, we chose the name Living Book instead of "writers' notebook" in our class. In our Living Books we jot down our observations and reflections of the previous day. This is where we store bits and pieces of our lives, bits and pieces we might miss if we didn't get it onto paper to be reread and revisited. When it's time to select a new writing topic, we look over our daily entries to discover or rediscover an event or observation to explore further in writing.

The Living Book is where kids write about being evacuated at 5:00 AM because a forest fire was cresting the ridge and threatening their apartment complex. It is where we record our observations of the sunset the previous night, what happened in soccer practice, what we heard in the news, what we're afraid of, new puppies, a new apartment with a room of your own, a fight with a family member, the book order getting here, worries about a sick pet. The Living Books store our observations of and responses to life.

The Teacher's Living Book

It is as useful for the teacher to keep a Living Book as it is for the kids, although in different ways and the topics might differ and the entries might be longer. In a Living Book the teacher can write observations of students and their actions and include personal reactions. This store of events and observations holds ideas to pursue in later lessons as well as records of good and bad times. Also, when you get to the point of exhaustion, it's a handy and wonderful reminder of why you are a teacher.

One day while going to pick the kids up after lunch recess, I looked out the window and watched Mitch and Steadman playing kickball with their friends. Steadman, in a walker because of cerebral palsy, was hauling himself to second base, laughing uproariously. The dust was flying as Mitch closed in on Steadman and nailed him with the ball.

In my Living Book I wrote:

A perfect Colorado day. A perfect Colorado recess. Blue sky, mountains crisp and clean in the distance. I looked down from the window and watched the kickball game on the playground. Steadman was on first base edging with his walker toward second. I laughed. That kid was full of spunk and energy. The ball was rolled and the kick went into center field where Mitch caught the ball.

Steadman, seeing Mitch catch the ball, began to scoot toward second base. Head back, laughing, he chugged toward second, dust flying. His helmet was rocking back and forth as he hustled to make it, Mitch closing in. Surely Mitch would give him a break; he was that kind of kid.

I watched Mitch slowly wind up with the ball, wind up to heave it at Steadman. Suspended, I watched, sure he would hesitate and throw gently. I watched as if in slow motion as Mitch let the ball go. The red ball spun and twisted until it nailed Steadman right in his back. A direct hit.

Steadman tumbled head over heels, his walker flying. I sucked in a breath. Was he all right? Would there be an argument? Mitch ran to retrieve the ball, ran back to retrieve the walker, and pulled Steadman back to his feet. From where I was, I couldn't quite tell if Steadman was laughing or crying, until I heard it. They clasped each other in a hug and roared with delight, friends. I could hear the laughter through the window. Friends.

I walked down the steps and out the door to retrieve them for music and gave Mitch a high five. "He nailed you buddy," I laughed at Steadman, "he nailed you. That was good, really good." Steadman looked at me, still laughing, and we walked into the building.

I wanted to capture that moment of true friendship. I wanted a record of Mitch treating Steadman as an equal, while showing his deep affection. I wanted that little piece of our class history.

The Living Book is a great place to store a lot of classroom history, to make note of the beautiful things kids routinely do. My Living Book carries the record of events such as these:

* Daniel brought in a Boy Scout compass for Sam because Sam was distraught at losing his. Daniel had an extra one and knew Sam would need it for his dream of building his own boat someday
* The first poem Nick wrote in his own Living Book
* The first time Taylor didn't roll her eyes when I disciplined her
* The first time that Preston shared his writing
* Hope's joyful playing in the Glenwood Springs pool during our field trip

My Living Book stores the newspaper articles I find so fascinating but never know what to do with. It contains the article about the Anasazi Indians at Mesa Verde building huge water reservoirs hundreds of years ago, articles about the reintroduction of wolves into the mountains of southern Colorado, articles about historic preservation, and recipes for dinners with friends. It's a place to store, in a way that doesn't junk up my life, all the things I find fascinating.

Joanne Hindley (1996, p. 18) has a long list of things that can be included in her writers' notebooks. After rereading her book, I expanded the notion of what goes in a Living Book to include the following:

* Questions you wonder about
* Memories
* Overheard conversations

* Images that stick in your mind
* Lists
* Family stories
* Interviews
* Opinions on issues and situations
* Responses to literature
* Plans for a project
* Quotations

Because the main purpose of our Living Books is to grow new topics, when we are working on self-selected topics, we review our Living Books for seeds of writing that we want to grow into bigger pieces. We look for interesting tidbits that are hiding in the backs of our minds. We look for trends in our writing over the previous months; what topics surface repeatedly. We search for a topic that was set aside for lack of time or a piece of writing that is ready to be published. We recall events in our lives to write about. We check to see if enough time has passed to write about a hurtful event. The entries are as varied as the students.

Jordan checks to see if enough time has passed to write about his parents' recent divorce. Hope wonders if she can write yet about the pain of not hearing from her brother for five months. Steadman writes about the *Titanic*. Taylor tries writing about the death of her dog again, to see if she get on paper the emotions and raw heartbreak that came from his passing. Nick writes about his Nintendo game. Tyler shares about changing classrooms in the middle of the year and how happy he is now. Shawn returns to his version of a Captain Underpants comic strip, again.

Gina exclaims over Easter:

"Yes! I finaly Easter!" I yelled. I got tons of candy. We found all the eggs. Mom and dad suck at hiding eggs!" I got the carebear Wishbear, I got bunny socks, gum and Strawberry Shortcake lip-gloss. I LOVED Easter!
    Gina

Nick writes down things he's learning about life:

One rain drop rasis the sea. Two rain drops rasis the lake and keeps the waterfall gong. You live to eat don't eat to live. Others first self last.

Weapons are enemys even to their owners. Those are the codes of dino-topiea. The moive.
    Nick

The Living Book documents things as they happen, like the fast-breaking TV news. It's quick snippets of life that can be revisited if an author chooses and when an author chooses.

Starting the day with Living Books sets the tone for the day . . . beginning with writing . . . makes space for kids to write about their lives. For the teacher, it's a way to begin the day peacefully, calmly.

Introducing Living Books

I recommend taking some time to introduce Living Books to the class. I show the kids examples of the type of empty journal they should get. Hindley (1996) emphasizes that the books should be very special so the writing is housed in something that signifies its importance. Beautiful blank books can be found at Wal-Mart, at grocery stores, and at bookstores. I set a deadline a couple of weeks away and write a letter about bringing in their blank books and send it home.

Many kids cannot afford a fancy writers' notebook so I purchase a lot of large composition notebooks. So the books will be special, the students create covers to reflect their personalities. Clear packing tape secures the covers to the composition notebooks and protects them from being torn.

When I introduce Living Books, the kids are not allowed to write in their books right away. Each day for two weeks, I model what entries should look like. To keep them from thinking these are diaries, I keep making mention of that fact. This writing will be vital, and it is to be cherished. These books will be much more than diaries; they will be life logs.

Before the kids begin their Living Books, I want them to see as many different people modeling writing as possible. For example, my model writing topics include the first days of the new year, the heat that wouldn't let go of Colorado, wildflowers, and the sunsets smeared with orange and red as a result of forest fires. To show the kids a different model, Dawn and I have traded classes. Dawn verbally processes as she writes, talking about the purpose and the motivation behind her writing. Dawn wrote about baseball, her passion, and about the exploits of her two sons as they pursued college baseball. Our principal came in to write with us. She wrote about her parents' upcoming fiftieth wedding anniversary, about her son's going to college, and about her daughter's being part of the Castle Rock Police Department junior officers division.

The kids are soon itching to write in their Living Books, but I'll have none of that. I use reverse psychology, knowing that if they don't get to begin right away, they will be overjoyed about writing when they do get the chance. After a couple of weeks of building suspense, they can begin to write entries, but on notebook paper, not in their Living Books. These entries I collect because I want to gradually release control to the kids by providing examples of what I am looking for from the kids, in addition to the examples they saw written by adults.

Following the gradual release of responsibility model, I begin turning over the sharing to selected kids based on the entries that have been collected the previous day. I choose selections that illustrate observations about life, that show incredible detail, that note something important—not entries that sound like a diary. I am sure to choose a lot of entries from reluctant writers because, honestly, they have some of the best reflections. Sometimes from these writers come simple, unexpected, profound thoughts. There is a conscious effort to make sure it isn't only the "good writers" who are asked to share.

Finally, the class has permission to write in the Living Books. It is incredible. The tone is reverent. The classroom is silent as we write, then when kids are directed to take a minute to jot down any other ideas they don't want to forget, the classroom bursts into noise. I encourage them to capture the moment before it is lost. They have a brief chance to get the essence of their experience on paper. Many kids return to an entry made the previous the day because it is an important idea that needs exploration.

Living Books Day by Day

When the hubbub of gathering and trivial tasks is behind us, we meet in the Oval Office, our Living Books in hand, and sit in a circle. I open by framing our learning and purpose for the day, then give a gentle reminder of the purpose of our Living Books:

Good morning. I'm so glad you're here. We have a very busy day. Today as you begin to write in your Living Books, let me remind you of their importance. This is a place for your life observations, a place to store the parts of you that make you you. This is not *a place for random doodling unless there is a purpose to those illustrations. I want you to be able to revisit your life as an adult and see what you thought about as a ten-year-old. This is to be a reminder of who you are, who you were. This is important. It's our place to plant seeds and grow new topics, and I want you to take this seriously.*

I don't know about you, but today I will have to spend at least some of my time writing about our Valentine's Day party on Friday. I want to remember the look on Jazmin's face when she had the icing on her nose, and I don't want to forget how cool Nick's box was that looked like Sponge Bob because Sponge Bob is so popular right now, but won't be later. It'll be something you will remember from your childhood. I also want to write about the snow this weekend, how absolutely soft and beautiful it was. It was something I don't want to forget, so I need to get it down before I lose it.

The comments about what the teacher might write about usually gets the wheels turning in the kids' heads for their writing.

The Living Books are for their eyes only. I never collect these books, never assess them, never evaluate them. This is their free writing time, their time to experiment in a nonthreatening way. This is the place for incomplete thoughts and sentences, for illustrations of the sunset and of the snow on our first field trip, for sketches of their Halloween costumes.

Sometimes it's necessary to intervene and redirect the kids. A couple of months ago, I noticed many of the kids doodling in their books, those weird line doodles all kids do. I reinforced for a week that the illustrations in their books should support the text, and that illustrations need text to explain the significance of the piece and the event that precipitated the need to illustrate something. I review the purpose of the Living Book and why we're spending the time on them.

On crazy days like Valentine's Day or before special events, on those days when the kids are distracted and off task, I circulate and give feedback. The kids sometimes need a reminder that we take this seriously, that it is not an option to write nothing. If they have nothing to write about, they write about having nothing to write about. Sometimes I have to jog their memories, to remind them of the countless stories they tell as they enter the classroom in the morning.

Each day we write from ten to twenty minutes. Then we share. It's a consistent procedure in the room. Sometimes I ask for volunteers to share their writing. Other days I ask to hear from people who haven't shared for a while. Sometimes we do a Whip Around: students select one line from anywhere in their own Living Books to share, and we whip around the circle, each student quickly sharing one line.

Other days, we look for trends. Students reread their recent entries or read their entire Living Books to see if there are trends, if there are recurrent themes that could be explored. I realized through my own book that many of my passages were about stress. It was shocking to see how much of my writing was about the stress I'd been feeling while trying to keep up, trying to get paperwork finished and grading done. It was a wake-up call to see that I was wasting so much of my professional life being stressed.

Trends in third and fourth graders' writing are:

* Cartoons
* Sleepovers
* Birthday presents
* Classroom events
* Family events, vacations
* Brothers and sisters

Trends in sixth graders' writing are:

* Conflicts with friends
* Issues of fitting in, not knowing their place in life
* Girls and boys
* Dating
* Friends at the Rec Center
* Fears and anxiety about going middle school

The amount of poetry written in Living Books might be surprising. It shouldn't be shocking, though, because they are a safe place to write.

Growing New Topics in the Living Books

When the time comes to select a new topic, we review our Living Books, looking for topics that beg for more time. To model doing this, in front of the kids, I go back through my Living Book and list topics that are still intriguing. Because I shared much of this with the kids as entries were written, this is schema for them, and they usually react and talk about it. Recently, my list looked like this:

Ohio vacation with Dad
Stress of conferences and report cards
Forest fire in Daniel's Park and the evacuations
RATS—2nd part to my "Not the Usual Summer" manuscript about
    moving into the house with all the rats
Mesa Verde nonfiction piece about what happened to the Anasazi

Once the list is assembled, I model how to select a topic by going down the list and exploring each topic orally in front of the kids, thinking aloud about each topic, seeing if it is worth writing about. Using the list above, I talk to the students in the following way:

My trip to Ohio was memorable because I saw more examples of how much my father loves me, but how he has trouble showing me. This would be a really important topic to write about since it is so recent and so heartfelt. If you remember, my dad is a minister and an all-around funny guy. He always started each sermon with a funny anecdote to get the congregation involved with his message for the day. I don't want to forget that incident, so this topic begs to have me write more about it.

The stress of report cards and conferences is sure on my mind, but I don't really want to write about that since it's just a fact of life. I mean, what would I write about? All I'd have to say is that I'm stressed, and to get over it and do it. That's it. It would be boring and wouldn't have any lasting impact on my life. So what if I'm stressed? I won't be after they're finished, so I'm going to cross that topic off the list. It was important in my Living Book, but it's done now. There's no reason to write more about it, and frankly, it would be a boring piece.

Now, the Daniel's Park forest fire was incredible. If you remember, we suddenly saw the smoke from our classroom window. You all ran over to the window yelling and screaming. We watched as more and more smoke billowed into the air, so we knew it was a big fire, not just a grass fire or a home fire. If you remember, you were worried about your own apartments and your parents, and you wondered if they knew about it. I wondered if the Pines Apartment kids would be able to go home because it looked so close to them, and I wondered if we'd be able to leave school. That would be a great topic to write about since it was so recent, so scary, and something we all experienced together.

I continue making my thinking clear because I'm modeling how an author makes choices. Since my kids usually know all of these topics from the daily sharing of Living Books, they become very involved with my choice. As I talk about each piece and its potential for writing, they voice their opinions.

To the dismay of some kids, I decided that for this piece, I would write about my dad. I was modeling, and one thing I was modeling was that some stories are so much a part of who we are that they only need to be put on paper. The rat story is part of who I am and has been told so many times, I have it memorized. The vacation with my dad was new and needed more time. I wanted the class to see why I chose that topic because it's what writers do.

Choices should generally be based on the needs of the whole class. It's good for them to see a model of writing about family in sensitive ways. It's good to push the depth of their writing, and writing about vacation with dad would do that.

Student Selection of Topics

When students begin their topic selection, they can follow the same procedure—go through their Living Books and make lists of topics they could write more about. In pairs they can talk with each other about that topic, exploring it to see if there is something more to write. Many times students pick interesting topics, but once they're into writing the piece, they find very little to write.

Because of this, it's a good idea to have students select their top three choices and do quick writes on each topic. The kids write for ten timed minutes on each topic, and they write as quickly as they can to get out as much about the topic as possible in that brief time. This helps to frame their thinking before they select a topic, and it helps with their planning once they lock into one topic.

Sometimes the kids realize there just isn't much to write about. Josiah wanted to write a piece about Nintendo but realized during the quick write that he didn't really have much to write about his Nintendo other than that he likes it and it's fun. Instead, he chose to write about stealing. He had been busted the previous week for stealing from other kids in the room, and he was still living with that shame. He faced the shame and shared his thinking with the class, and in doing so, made friends and cleared his name.

The excitement of Living Book time sometimes fades and needs an infusion of energy. That's the time to bring in a popular teacher to share his or her writing. A new face and voice perks up interest. Or I'll ask for volunteers to donate lines from their Living Books and put them on the wall. I want this time to be different, special.

We are very lucky to have a guru of Living Books who teaches in the district. Her name is Randi Allison, and she volunteers to come and share her Living Books with us. One day she came tromping in, dragging behind her a large suitcase on wheels. Her shocking red hair is reason alone for amazement, but when she opened that suitcase, the kids gasped. The suitcase was filled with Living Books, representing every phase of her life. She spent the morning with us, talking about how important the Living Books were to her life.

She made a huge impact of the importance of the Living Books to her when she asked the kids to give her a day, a month, and a year. One student would call out a date like June 17, 1999. She'd sift through the suitcase, find the appropriate book, and read the passage for the corresponding date. For days when she hadn't written anything, she'd say, "Ohhhhh, I'm sorry. But the events of that day have escaped forever because I don't have it written down."

When there was a passage written for the given date, she read out what was written and shared her reactions. For January 16, 1993, the day she had learned that her daughter, Jennifer, was pregnant, she read:

January 16, 1993
Last night I felt a miracle.
Her soft, smooth belly rippled,
my hand jumped, tears filled my eyes.
I felt the miracle
twitter here, twitter there
swimming here and swimming there.
Tumbling, twisting, turning.
pushing, stretching
demanding to greet me.
Last night I felt a miracle.

Randi's eyes filled with tears as she reflected on the events of that joyous day. The kids were touched. They got it. Randi would never forget that moment, but had it not been written in Randi's Living Book, the exact feeling may have been lost . . . forever.

Living Books are one way to set the tone for the writers' workshop. Living Books are one answer to student selection of writing topics. The students have a wealth of topics they can write about. Since I have begun writing Living Books, I don't hear "I don't know what to write" as much. Planting the seeds of our lives is part of our daily writing routine.

5

Modeling Writing

I need to model writing for my kids. Through my modeling I verbalize what writers do. The thought of writing in front of our kids brings fear to many teachers, who feel more comfortable modeling their thinking in reading than in writing. It is no surprise that kids feel the same way— more comfortable reading than writing.

How ironic that most kids enter school knowing they can write and can't read, and we turn that around through repeated failure and frustration. Writing is hard for many people because it involves so many thinking processes that go beyond the actual manipulation of the language.

I know why most teachers are reluctant to write publicly . . . because I was too. I was afraid to write because I was not a C. S. Lewis. Or a Patricia MacLachlan. Or a Sharon Creech. Or a Gary Paulsen. Heck, I wasn't even a writer for the *National Enquirer*! I was just an ordinary guy from a small town in Ohio with ordinary experiences. Not even if paid a million dollars could I come up with a line like, "with all that new breathing in the house," which Cynthia Rylant wrote in *The Relatives Came*.

Who could match the prose of Kate DiCamillo in *Because of Winn-Dixie* (2001, pp. 94–95)?

"Look at this tree," Gloria said.

I looked up. There were bottles hanging from just about every branch. There were whiskey bottles and beer bottles and wine bottles all tied on with string, and some of them were clanking against each other and making a spooky kind of noise. Me and Winn-Dixie stood and stared at the tree, and the hair on top of his head rose up a little bit and he growled deep in his throat.

Gloria Dump pointed her cane at the tree.

"What do you think about this tree?"

I said, "I don't know. Why are all those bottles on it?"

"To keep the ghosts away," Gloria said.

"What ghosts?"

"The ghosts of all the things I done wrong."

I looked at all the bottles on the tree. "You did that many things wrong?" I asked her.

"Mmmmm-hmmmm," said Gloria. "More than that."

"But you're the nicest person I know," I told her.

"Don't mean I haven't done bad things," she said.

Most of us cannot match that kind of writing, but we don't have to. Most of us will never win the Pulitzer Prize, the Newbery Medal, or any other writing award. Yet we are real, living, breathing writers all the same. We write to capture our lives, and that's what our students need to see us model.

We don't need to know everything about the text features of the different genres and write fluently and magnificently in all of them to teach them well. Every piece of work we produce needn't have lasting power, needn't stand out in the kids' minds or move them emotionally. We don't have to be terrific writers from the start; we can be writers who improve.

It's not a bad thing if the teacher's writing grows and evolves during the year. We should expect to grow as writers, just as we expect our kids to grow because we will grow as a result of our writing together. If we give ourselves permission to take risks and to struggle with writing in front of the kids— to experiment and revise and play with words— the students will see someone living the writing life.

They need to know that a lot of writing is truly bad, but once in a while we stumble on a gem. It's perfectly all right to produce horrible writing while working on new ideas and techniques. They need to see the tension of the race to publishing deadlines, the sweat spent in getting a piece finished in time for the author celebration. It's much easier talking with the kids and working with them when we are rushing toward a publishing deadline together.

What It Looks Like

When writing with kids, it's important to keep many things in mind while structuring the writing sessions. First, the physical arrangement. We gather in the Oval Office. The closeness strengthens the community and the intimacy, and the teacher can easily monitor their engagement and attentiveness. I have a seating chart for the kids who need it, having them right at my feet so I can tap them on the head for attention. The other kids sit wherever they like in this tight cluster.

They can bring nothing with them that might be distractions, and all the materials for the lesson are right there for easy access. The chart paper is right next to my comfortable chair and the lamp. All the picture books that I will use for the week are propped up on the chart stand, and there are mugs of markers next to them. It's very cozy.

Tips for Modeling Writing
* Write about what you know.
* Write from the heart.
* Be open to suggestions from the kids, and they'll be open to you.
* Cozy up and make it intimate, an event the kids look forward to and will want to be part of.

When I model writing, my planning for the piece is almost always done on chart paper. I think aloud as I model this planning. Later I model organizing the mess of ideas listed on the paper. I use this draft of ideas for my entire piece, going back to the planning so the kids see how I use the plan to structure the writing. I also spend a lot of time revising the PLAN, which I think is vital, because the piece changes as I write it.

I write a lot about my childhood in Ohio. One of my favorite topics to write about is about Clyde Caulkins, the bully mentioned in Chapter 1. It was Clyde's sole job to relieve every kid of spare change daily. He was in our fifth-grade classroom, although I swear he drove a car to school. I distinctly remember he had his own parking place; he was that big and that old. It was his fifth time in fifth grade. The mere mention of his name could evoke crying in the hallway from any kid in school. I'm sure by now that he's a full-time member of the Ohio Penal Commission, though I don't know that to be true.

As I talk about Clyde and begin to write about him, the kids warm to the topic, amazed there were bullies way back then. They love any tales from my years as a tween. My writing spurs their writing about bullies. My exaggerations create a sense of playfulness in the classroom that comes from sharing life. We laugh together as I write about how big he was, how green his teeth were, how much money I lost to that guy.

Here is the planning chart for my story about Clyde, "Monster in the Town":

* That voice, booming down the hall "Hey, Morgan!"
* Oldest fifth-grade kid in the history of Jonathan Alder School District
* Felt him coming, felt his very presence, every hair on the back of my neck felt it
* Close calls—repeatedly
* Friends told me he was after me—dead meat; checking the hallway before leaving school, no Clyde
* Alley—the demilitarized zone in Plain City, Ohio, there he was
* Money, he wanted it all
* 25 cents every time I saw him after that
* Paper route bankruptcy because of Sopranos-type blackmail
* Felt like a disgrace

It's good to model writing something every day. I start planning and writing a piece with the class and add a couple of paragraphs each day. I continue writing after school, print that segment, and share it the next day. The kids can observe the process, the composing and the thinking that accompany the writing of the piece.

When sharing the writing done away from the class, I print a copy in large font so the kids can see the writing. Then I can talk about why something was included and something else wasn't. I model various writing techniques. For example, I talk about compressing time to keep the audience's attention; the writing doesn't include every detail like, "And then I went to bed and I slept for eight hours. When I woke up, I put on my socks and shoes and had a smoothie for breakfast after feeding the dogs." You get the picture.

I sit in my comfortable chair, using the chart paper and computer printouts of my overnight efforts. Other teachers model on strips of paper and mount them on the wall. Some teachers use the overhead projector so they can face the classroom all the time to monitor engagement. It's a matter of personal style.

I prefer to have the students right in front of me instead of at their desks. Especially when I begin, the kids are not totally engaged and paying attention as I write. They are expected to pay attention so they can try to approximate what has been modeled for them. I constantly reinforce the purpose for writing with them—that good writers learn from other writers. When the model lesson is finished, they return to their desks and try to apply what they have seen modeled. As a result of the continual focus on the purpose of modeling, I expect student engagement to increase over time. I verbally reward students who are participating, by listening, adding their ideas, and making them the stars. There are years when this doesn't happen, but I never waver on its importance.

Through it all, I talk about writing, about what I'm struggling with, what isn't going right, where I'm stuck. I ask for their help in clarifying, always checking to see if I've given them enough knowledge and explaining when something was purposely left hanging, which requires them to infer.

The writing demonstration is part of the writing block. The kids know to gather at the same time every day, like clockwork. It's part of our routine, and it's one of our procedures that does not change. The kids expect it, and it sets the tone for their writing time after they return to their seats for composing time.

Choosing Topics to Model Writing

Many teachers wonder about what type of writing to model for their kids. At Castle Rock, we model from life—our own and the classroom life we share with kids. We write about the trivial things we take for granted, things the kids know about. It helps students to see that we are surrounded by the stuff of good writing.

For example, I often write about my dogs. Since I am single, my dogs are my kids, my companions, and the source of countless stories. When I first brought my new puppy Gladys home from the rescue league, the class couldn't wait to hear about her latest exploits in my writing. They were relieved that I had a new puppy because they had also through previous writing cried with me as I put my beloved fifteen-year-old dog, Miguel, to sleep. They felt with me as I'd write about going home, grabbing the dog food bowl by habit, and realizing she wasn't there anymore. They celebrated as I wrote about going to the rescue league. They wanted me to have that puppy more than I did. They knew the story and had the schema to understand exactly what I was feeling.

They waited anxiously to see how I'd get Gladys to stop crying and howling when I put her to bed. That dog just didn't want to give up. She was like a belligerent kid refusing to go to bed. The kids offered solutions that I would try that night to get her to bed; solutions I would write about the next day. They loved the gross stories I'd write about, those moments when I'd wake from a dead sleep, scrambling for a tee shirt to get under her mouth before she threw up on the carpet. I made sure to write vividly about that retching noise only dog and cat owners can know, that noise that can rouse you from a deep sleep and have you involuntarily searching for something to protect that new carpet. I write about my dogs because the kids *know* this too.

They loved to hear about my Dalmatian, Cody, and my getting him from the dog pound minutes before he was put to sleep. They knew every grueling detail as I wrote about his slicing the end of his tail off on the chain link fence when I went to pick him up. He was ecstatic to see a human.

Tweens all have pet stories, all have loved pets, and if they don't have a pet, they *want* one. Pet stories are a shoe-in. I always think back to college when friends would come to our off-campus house to get my dog. "Babe magnet," they'd mutter as they took her toward the College Commons. "Everybody likes a dog," they'd continue. My college friends knew it then, and my kids know it now.

Taking Risks with Writing

By the time tweens reach us, some are already outcasts. Rejected by peers or adults, they have already coarsened and are building up a hard exterior shell. Writing may be an avenue to reach these tough kids.

A couple of years ago, Cliff entered the room. I had already heard about Cliff from his previous teachers, and knew I was in for a ride. In our first parent/teacher conference, his mother bet me a six-pack of beer that he wouldn't work, wouldn't do homework, and wouldn't learn. I bet her he would.

Cliff walked into the room along with his reputation. I sent him to the hallway in the first ten minutes of school on the first day, not a good sign during that honeymoon grace period. One of the students, Monica, looked at me knowingly and said, "Get used to it, he's out there a lot." In fact, he was kicked out of our first-day all-school assembly, an assembly with an agenda of reinforcing behavioral and conduct expectations!

He had one of those voices that carries for a mile. No matter what he was doing, he was loud. By the end of that first day, I snapped and was yelling at him in the hallway, shaking my finger in his face. Luckily, I realized in the midst of my tirade that I was the adult and said, "Cliff, I'm sorry. I'm being a real jerk. I don't mean to . . ."

He cut me off saying, "No, I'm the jerk. Ask them in there," he said gesturing to the classroom, "They know. They've lived with me for a while." My heart melted then. The kids knew him already, they knew he was always in trouble, but they weren't able to see his big heart and that he was a sweet, gentle kid. I wanted to write about it in an honest way.

Something inspired me to write about Cliff and his behavior, good and bad, showing both the tough and gentle sides of him. It would certainly be an interesting topic that the kids knew, and it might engage Cliff in the writing workshop.

"You know, Cliff, I've got an idea . . . what would you think if I wrote about this . . . wrote about this with your help. What would you think if you helped me plan my piece and sat with me as I wrote? It might allow the kids in the room to see a different side of you, the side I see that may not be as obvious to kids. I think it may be a way to change some ideas in there."

Cliff was ecstatic. He would get the chance to be noted for something, to be counted.

This was risky for Cliff and me. You have to be very careful with this type of topic because it can damage kids badly if not handled well. After Cliff and I talked privately and began the planning, I could see that it would turn out all right to use him as a subject for model writing with the class.

I started my writing demonstration the next day in front of the kids. I was very firm that the kids couldn't add their own stories about Cliff. This wasn't going to be open season on Cliff. There was a purpose to my writing, and it was not to bash Cliff.

Each day, I would write for ten to fifteen minutes in front of them while sharing my planning, my thinking, my revisions, and constantly checking with them to see if my writing was clear. I would enlist their help as we wrote this story together, and I remembered exactly what they had said. The entire time, though, they knew that I respected Cliff and that I would accept only respect for him.

Again, after the kids left, I'd write more on the computer and then would share the writing the next day. Here is the start of the text I wrote:

The Big Boil

I love the first day of school, it's so invigorating, so clean, so full of promise. The kids are actually nice, well-behaved and polite. Teachers in the lounge talk about how great their classes are, how reserved, how easy to work with, how much they pay attention. It's the honeymoon period.

My kids filed in, clean and shiny in their new clothes, backpacks full of brand new supplies. Quiet. They were so quiet. The whole school was quiet. That is until I heard a commotion in the hallway. I heard a loud laugh, heard this kid yelling to everyone and joking with everyone. I must have had a puzzled look on my face because Monica pointed to the hallway and muttered, "Cliff."

"What, Monica?" I asked.

"Cliff. It's Cliff. He's in our room. He's been in my room for four years now. It's Cliff."

"Oh, Cliff," I nodded, the stories flooding my mind. Cliff had a legacy. Cliff was a legacy.

We continued writing together, making sure to get those great quotes into the piece. We made sure to record Monica's exact words, "Get used to it, Mr. Morgan. Believe me, I've lived it . . . lived it all . . . four years in the same classroom as him. I've lived it ALLLLLLLL!"

I also made public that in many ways Cliff was a regular kid, even if he could be a real pain. They already knew that, believed that he was worse than a pain. Writing about Cliff did not create an open season for him that year. It created the expectation that Cliff was an amazing kid, capable of growth and love, and told the kids firmly that I expected to see changes in him that year.

Writing to Build Community

Sometimes it's fun to write with students about experiences we have shared. When I was the reading resource teacher for the intermediate grades, I'd go into classrooms for demonstrations and small-group work.

I walked into Marla Applegate's fourth-grade classroom one day and shot her a glance. She flashed me a blank stare and we burst into laughter. We were desperate with this group. They were flat and lifeless. Nothing we did seemed to shake them from their complacency. We were at the point where we were sure the whole year would be that way. Here it was November and nothing we had done so far had sparked enthusiasm, involvement, or excitement. We felt trapped.

That day, though, things were about to change. Marla had just tracked back on after a three-week break and was frustrated that while she was gone somebody had stolen her chart stand and replaced it with a rickety, lame structure. She was incensed that her overhead had been replaced, too, with one that was so dirty you couldn't focus it clearly. (Recall that in our year-round school, one teacher leaves for vacation and is replaced by a teacher tracking back on. When a teacher goes out, everything in the room has to be taken down, packed into carts, and moved out. The chaos is amazing. Things get lost, things get taken, things get traded while you're gone.)

When I saw the flimsy chart stand, I immediately donned my Superman cape and went into my fix-it routine. My favorite part of the Sunday newspaper is the Home Depot ads. I pore through them as soon as the paper arrives, planning my next project. So it was no surprise I was excited about the fix-it project. It was surprising, though, that the classroom erupted into activity to help fix the stand and the overhead.

Soon the entire classroom was involved in the renovations to the stand and the overhead. We were laughing and playing together to solve the dilemma. In the midst of the happy chaos, Marla yelled, "We need to write about this." The kids groaned. But we pulled the kids to the newly stable chart stand and began to write about our time together.

It was perfect. The kids were thrilled we were writing about them, and they were eager to tell us exactly what they had said and how they had been involved in the process. That classroom had finally come alive!

We published the piece, typing it on the computer in a large font, and then printed it so each student could illustrate one page. We displayed the manuscript on the wall around the room and referred to it as part of our shared history.

I am always alert for moments shared with students to write about together. When we took a walking field trip to our new town library, I wrote about the trip. I wrote about pushing Hope's wheelchair down the hill and all the way to the library because it was too cold for her to operate the controls. The kids relived the countless times her shawl wrapped around the wheels. Once inside the library, I slowed down the time sequence when Jake made it into the revolving door (a new phenomenon in Castle Rock), but his backpack didn't; it got stuck between the frame and the door!

Simple, everyday events. Events we take for granted—the stuff of good writing, if we're lucky enough to recognize it.

Postscript

Because you're a teacher and spend your life worrying about kids, many of you may be wondering what happened to Cliff. I know you want to hear about a beautiful ending, that he turned it all around and became a star student. Sigh.

One day, Cliff didn't come to school. I felt the euphoria that we might have a smooth day, but first I checked with the kids to see if he was in the office for being in trouble on the bus. The kids assured me he wasn't, that he hadn't gotten on at his stop. I began to worry because Cliff would have showed up in the middle of the Bubonic Plague. If we had a snow day, Cliff still came to school because he loved being there. Something was up.

An hour later, accompanied by the principal, he showed up at the classroom door. Cliff's face looked anxious and worried; the principal's looked stern and grave. "Mr. Morgan," she began after calling me to the door, "Please take some time to reinforce with Cliff the gravity of the situation this morning. Cliff missed the bus and hitchhiked the seventeen miles here because he didn't want to miss school. Please remind him of the dangers he faced in doing this, even though it was commendable that he did so." Secretly, she looked over the top of his head and broke into a huge grin, leaving me to keep it serious.

That kid. We had an eventful year. He ended the year with friends, which was a major accomplishment for him. He was able to let the kids in the room see the beauty inside, and they welcomed him into their lives.

I still laugh about our times together. I still love that kid. I still hear from him occasionally. And I have it on paper. Forever.

6

Mentor Texts

We didn't always live on Mango Street. Before that we lived on Loomis on the third floor, and before that we lived on Keeler. Before Keeler it was Paulina, and before that I can't remember. But what I remember most is moving a lot . . .

They always told us that one day we would move into a house, a real house that would be ours for always so we wouldn't have to move each year. And our house would have running water and pipes that worked. And inside it would have real stairs, not hallway stairs, but stairs inside like the houses on T.V. And we'd have a basement and at least three washrooms so when we took a bath we wouldn't have to tell everybody. Our house would be white with trees around it, a great big yard, and grass growing without a fence. This was the house Papa talked about when he held a lottery ticket and this was the house Mama dreamed up in the stories she told us before we went to bed.

But the house on Mango Street is not the way they told it at all. It's small and red with tight steps in front and windows so small you'd think they were holding their breath. Bricks are crumbling in places, and the

*front door is so swollen you have to push hard to get in. Out back is a
small garage for the car we don't own yet . . .*

Sandra Cisneros, *The House on Mango Street* (1991 pp. 3–4)

Windows so small you'd think they were holding their breath?
A garage for the car we don't own yet? When I finished
reading this signature piece from a collection of vignettes
by Sandra Cisneros, I had to share it with my kids at school so we could
write about it. This story prompted incredible schema connections.

The first morning, as I shared the text orally, I let the kids know that
I was on a hot topic and absolutely had to write about my connections. I
gasped as I made my way through it, sharing with them what great writing does in the mind of the reader, how it can take you someplace you've
never been, how it can create in you a writing place that you never knew
existed. The first day, all I did was read it orally, talking at length about
my connections.

The next day we gathered in the Oval Office and I reread this selection to them. While reading, I listed my schema connections to this piece,
recording on chart paper memories of a house not quite being what I had
expected. I outlined my memories of our first real house in Ohio, and
then I used the planning to model my writing for the next week. Each
day, following my writing outline, I wrote more and revised my writing
with students sitting in front of me, asking them for help to make sure I
was making my point clear.

The following essay is the writing that Sandra Cisneros inspired me
to write.

632 Maplecrest Drive
*We had always lived in sensible places, sensible places with sensible
names. The square boxes we called home were farm town practical, with
few frills and even less glamour, and they were perched on roads with
names that were equally no-nonsense and to the point. For the first sixteen years of my life, my addresses were solid names like Rural Route 2,
Richwood, Ohio. Or State Route 42, Plain City, or, when pushed, num-
bered streets like 535 5th Avenue, Waverly, Ohio.*

    *When I heard we were moving . . . yet again . . . I was filled with
dread. My third high school. Moving for my senior year. It was the kiss
of death socially. I was doomed to a year of no personal life; nobody would
care about somebody moving in the last year of high school.*

I was filled with dread until I heard the address. 632 Maplecrest Drive. 632. It sounded like poetry. And the street name. Oh, the street name. Maplecrest Drive. Maplecrest Drive. Not Maplecrest Street. Not State Route Maplecrest. Maplecrest Drive.

For the next three weeks, I pictured it in my mind. Pictured the white farmhouse with a wraparound porch, the winding lane leading up to a carriage house tucked behind. The views from the crest were breathtaking and, stretched from one hill to the next, fertile Ohio farmland reaching out as far as the eye could see.

The boughs of the maple trees stretched out, framing the house from the road, almost like a picture. These were real trees. Trees so old, so sturdy, so thick that you could pull yourself up into them and lie secure on the limbs as you gazed through the lush canopy of maple leaves. These were limbs where, in the heat of the summer, you could pull yourself up and lie with a good book, as the state sweltered around you.

I had grown up in church parsonages with pale pastel walls of light green and pink. Colors so washed out they weren't even colors. Good sensible colors that would fit the next minister too. I had grown up in church parsonages that didn't belong to us, so the walls remained unadorned.

Not 632 Maplecrest Drive. It was to be our first home. All ours. The wind coming up the ridge would blast through the windows and slam into walls that were splashed with too much red for a wall to stand. The yellow in the hallway would be so bright that you didn't need the light on to see. Our house. All ours. A place to call home. A place where we could live for more than three years.

As I sat in the car driving across the flatness of I-70 Ohio, I strained for a look at the sign announcing our new town. Finally it appeared. State route 201 Tipp City, Troy, Ohio. It was just as I pictured. The flatness of the heartland had given way to gently sloping hills, hills that led to crests shielded from the world by tall trees. I was coming home.

I saw the sign announcing Troy. Troy. Another grand name. Not Chuckery, Ohio. Not Plain City, Ohio. Troy. The grand, tree-lined boulevards led us to the downtown traffic circle, Erie Canal–era buildings gracing each corner. A huge fountain spouted from the center. We were home. This was a town, a real town. A real, classy town. No junked cars in front yards, no sofas on front porches. This place was class.

We traveled across the Miami River and onto Staunton Road. The high school, huge and imposing, sat on my left, awaiting my arrival.

Suddenly we turned. I was jerked into reality. "Where are we going?"
I demanded.

"This is our street," my dad relayed.

"What the . . ." I hollered, jerking my head back to the view
around me. Cookie-cutter little houses lined the street. Lined a street so
flat, so ordinary, it must be a mistake. "No, I mean, where is Maplecrest
Drive?" I asked again and again.

"This is it," my dad replied, his tone a little sharper.

"Where are the maples? Where's the hill? Where's the . . ."

"Bruce, this is IT!" he said firmly, a little less calmly. His "don't
make me come back there" glance in the rearview mirror silenced me,
at least for a while.

I looked helplessly around. To my dismay, he pulled the Ford
Country Squire station wagon into the last house before the four-way
stop. One tiny maple tree stood in the yard. ONE tiny Maple tree in the
exact spot as every other tree on the block. The bi-level house with a too-
big garage stood before us.

This can't be it. It must be some kind of joke. But it wasn't.
Everybody piled out of the car, excited to see our first real house. They
all struggled to get in the front door while I wandered into the backyard;
wandered into the backyard, for the huge trees, for the hill, for the
breeze. There were four small maples there, but no hill. There wasn't a
hill within a mile. There was a view all right, not of expansive terrain,
but of other houses just like ours separated by a chain-link fence.

632 Maplecrest Drive. I said it aloud, in disgust, and turned and
slunk to the front of the house to see where we would live for the rest of
tomorrow. 632 Maplecrest Drive.

When I finished reading my piece, the kids talked at length about their
own "Mango Street" experiences. They had stories that needed to be written, so they went back to their seats to write.

✳ ✳ ✳

Erin, a sixth grader, wrote of an abandoned property near her house that
tugs at her.

The Land
I pasted an abandoned house today, a barn and a shed, too. The house,
bar, and shed used to be new, with people, probably pilgrims inside,

*horses eating hay in the new barn, not getting out of the territory by the
new fence.*

Now the house is crumbling, windows, some holding their place.

*The barn with no hay, but ghosts of houses, horses at play. The fence
no longer holds its place, it's hanging by old posts, once new.*

*Take a look around, won't you, look at what we've done. This land
once happy, now has buildings, and roads, and all sorts of things.*

*This land, once happy, roamed with happy buffalo, now scarce with
fear.*

*Indians roamed this once happy land of ours, with tribes and chil-
dren, free animals, too.*

Take a look around, and see what we've done.

Take a look around and see what mess, we have begun.

Michael was thoughtful and introspective. He always had a slightly
different perspective, and the other sixth graders respected his gentle
nature.

My Special Place
My special place is more colorful than an art museum.
There is always music playing.
It smells like fresh-baked cookies.
If you licked it, it would taste like a sugary sucker.
It feels like a heavenly bed.
There are no criminals.
No questions unanswered.
No school; everybody knows everything . . .
No disabled people.
You can do anything you want to do.
It's like being in a fairy tale,
But you get more than three wishes.
No war exists.

When mentor texts are used to stimulate writers, their writing
improves. Various authors are introduced to the classroom as the experts;
their writing offers models of how to weave details through the text to
make the message clear, to present it in a certain way, to evoke responses
in readers.

I use beautiful interesting texts to study, admire, and imitate. I use mentor texts to stimulate our writing, add depth, or study new techniques challenges us as writers. As we practice, refine, revise, and improve, we can continually refer to our models, our mentors, to gauge our success. Mentor texts set benchmarks for us to strive to attain. They lead the way to new writing places.

I use the same texts many times throughout the year, and every time I read a favorite text again, the class finds new ways to use it. Because I choose beautiful text to study and imitate, I am free from the fear of needing my writing be a work of art. I am more conscious of being a writer, which frees me to demonstrate and coach my students.

Picture Books as Mentor Texts

Demonstrations of good writing can involve a variety of materials including poetry, newspaper articles, magazines, and novels. I feel compelled to use picture books, for many reasons. They bring a vividness that distinguishes them from other texts. The rich illustrations, the concise text, the repeating themes make them a natural for tween classrooms. It's surprising how many teachers think tweens won't react favorably to these books, fearing they'll be rejected because they're for little kids. They appeal on many levels, especially to tween poets and artists.

I love walking into middle school classrooms and telling the teachers that I'm pulling the kids to the front to demonstrate a strategy while using a picture book. In one classroom, the teacher replied, "That's fine and all, but you're on your own, buddy. I can't be responsible." Minutes later, she was flabbergasted as her students sat mesmerized.

My theory about picture books is that not a whole lot of kindergarteners can drop $15.00 on a picture book. Adults fall in love with the books and then buy them for their kids. Tweens get that. The rest is easy. Tween artists are mesmerized by the artwork, too, which is another hook to these books.

Teachers can use the text of picture books for a variety of purposes. They can be good discussion starters to get the kids engaged and talking. There are many provocative texts that are open-ended and ripe for discussion. Picture books can be used to connect reading strategies we are studying with writers' craft. The following table lists a few favorite picture books for use with tweens, along with their authors and the strategies they support.

Title	Author	Strategies
An Angel for Solomon Singer	Cynthia Rylant	Inferring, questioning visualization
The Relatives Came	Cynthia Rylant	Schema, beautiful language, inferring
The Seashore Book	Charlotte Zolotow	Schema
The Stranger	Chris Van Allsburg	Questioning, inference
The Old Woman Who Named Things	Cynthia Rylant	Questioning, schema, predictions
When I Was Young in the Mountains	Cynthia Rylant	Schema
What You Know First	Patricia MacLachlan	Schema, inferring
Now One Foot, Now the Other	Tomie dePaola	Inference

Most often, though, I use picture books to stimulate thinking that can be put into writing. As I read a book orally, I chart all the schema connections I'm making to the book, possibly to write about later. Also, I jot down ideas and later I choose some of them to develop in writing.

Kids think that when they write, it must be a masterpiece like *Walk Two Moons*, *Holes*, or *Where the Red Fern Grows*. They need constant reminders that the small incidents in life are the events we can all identify with, that audiences crave reading about regular, common events.

Picture books are a natural way to stimulate this thinking and writing. *The Scarecrow* by Cynthia Rylant is about living life simply, taking the time to allow animals to come to you and enjoy you for what you are. *The Tenth Best Thing About Barney*, by Judith Viorst, is about a young boy dealing with the death of his beloved cat. Tomie dePaola's *Nana Upstairs*, *Nana Downstairs* and *Now One Foot, Now the Other* are about young people dealing with aging.

We use some books repeatedly throughout the year, books likely to generate many schema connections in the kids. One of my all-time favorite books, a book that is as fresh the thousandth time as it was the first, is *The Relatives Came* by Cynthia Rylant. *The Relatives Came* can demonstrate a circular ending and it can show how time is recorded as the grapes in the book mature. It can show powerful writing with phrases like, "with all that new breathing in the house, and beds that were too big and too quiet" (Rylant 1993).

I use *The Relatives Came* first for a reading mini-lesson and then later for the writing mini-lesson. For example, I may begin the day with a reading crafting lesson on schema connections, demonstrating how good readers make connections to the text and identify with the people or events in the book. After the mini-lesson, the kids go to their scats for independent reading time to practice this strategy, to make schema connections from their reading to their lives. Later, the same book shows up in the writing demonstration because it's the book that sparks all the connections I chart while reading, connections I can then write about. Here is a plan for repeated use of *The Relatives Came*.

Ideas for Repeated Use of The Relatives Came

* Springboard for my own writing—make lists of connections.
* Time elements—reread to see how Rylant shows the passage of time.
* Choral reading—photocopy sheets, pair students.
* Powerful, unusual language—reread and chart new ways to say things.
* Circular endings—reread to demonstrate how some authors begin and end a book in the same way.

The kids are clustered in front of me as I compile a list of topics the book suggests. From the very beginning, this book just grabs me because it so reminds me of all the times relatives have visited me. I stop repeatedly to spin stories the reading brings up for me and remind students there are many connections to one text.

I jot as I talk. "On the first page, when the relatives talk about leaving behind their almost purple grapes, it reminds me of the time my friend Todd was in town from Portland. We sat under my backyard grape arbor one August day, looking at the purple grapes above us. Gazing up at those plump, scented grapes, he said, 'Why don't we make grape jelly today.'"

Todd's offer triggered a flood of memories, of steamy Ohio afternoons when my grandmother, grandfather, and mother would be bustling around the kitchen boiling grapes and putting up jars of grape jelly."

"Well," I continue, talking to the kids and jotting down notes, "it turned into a huge production that stretched into two days. Fifteen trips to different stores to find canning jars, lids, wax, cheesecloth, and the stand to hold the cheesecloth, resulted in bags of supplies." I stress that I am the kind of person who has to do things exactly right, that if I don't, it's sure to fail. I was sure if I didn't have all the exact supplies, the jelly would be ruined, and that created undue stress that day.

"Then, of course, it didn't gel, which meant trips around the neighborhood checking with friends to see if they had any suggestions. It turned into a neighborhood affair, with four people giving us four different ideas. We set off to the store again to get pectin, which was sure to change everything."

By this point, the kids are roaring, and I keep jotting down notes. I can exaggerate as well as anyone, so I demonstrate how this helps the writing, how it brings interest and humor to a story. I tell them that $2,000 later, we had the jars of jelly ready to store in the basement.

The next day, we look at the book again and continue making schema connections. I read the page where the kids in the book are sitting, waiting for the relatives to come. That day, I write about the times in Ohio when I'd wait outside on the front steps, waiting, and waiting, and waiting for my relatives. My grandfather was my hero, my savior. He was my best friend. I'd sit and wait, just like the kids in *The Relatives Came*, until I saw my grandfather's Chevy turn down the street. I'd jump up, run into the house, and scream, "They're here!" and then I'd race back outside and tear down the block to meet them. My great-aunt would always be in the back, my grandmother in the front, purse always perched primly in her lap. Auntie would begin to wave furiously as I raced them back down the sidewalk and into the driveway.

And then the hugging, oh the hugging. Hugging all around until my grandmother's fingers would slowly travel in an intentional move to my cheek, for the Grandmother Cheek Pinch and the reassuring, "You are growing like a weed."

Again, the kids are engaged and want to tell their stories. Marina shares her excitement that her grandparents are coming at Christmas time and that they spoil her to death. She knows that for the week of their visit she gets to eat ice cream every night. Jake tells about all the times he goes fishing with his grandpa. His grandparents are coming in the spring and he'll get to fish with grandpa as much as he likes. Shawn tells us that his grandmother lives right by the school, which is great when he gets sick because she is right there. As they talk, I jot down these reflections as well, so we can access them later.

I chart my thinking and their ideas quickly, trying to get down the main points before they're forgotten. I explain the need to get thoughts out in the drafting process, to get them out as quickly as possible; we can come back later to organize, reflect, and revise.

Continuing through *The Relatives Came*, we make more connections to the story. The scene where all the relatives are eating reminds me of

Thanksgiving at my grandfather's house. Kids were banished to card tables in a pecking order of importance. My older brother got to sit at the card table, and I was stuck with one of those stupid metal TV trays with the huge painted roses on it, roses faded beyond recognition. I tell them about the first time he got to sit at the big table with the real people, and he gloated about it the entire way from home to my grandfather's. Way before it was time to eat, he took his place, making sure we all saw him sitting high and mighty at the big table, and continually looking over at us peons and sneering.

As I exaggerate, students are talking with their friends about similar experiences. I ask them to predict the ending, although they are unable to predict the cruel twist of fate that day. I build the story to the point that the kids are begging to find out what happens in the end. I reveal the glorious close to the story.

Mister High and Mighty, on his fortieth time sneering back at us, got caught by our dad. "Ronald, this table invitation was not done for the purpose of your gloating. Kids, scoot around and make room for your brother at the card table. We'll try this arrangement again next year." The classroom roars with glee; the villain gets his just punishment. I continue jotting down notes as I talk, notes of all the topics the kids were talking about as I talked, and then they go to their seats to write about their own schema connections.

We achieve many things by doing this together. Some kids are so turned off by writing because of repeated failure that they have no concept of writing as a pleasant experience. These shared oral experiences provide positive constructs for successful, enjoyable writing. These shared writing times also build community. Students get a glimpse of my life through these times and get to see me as a writer writing about small slices of life. I want the kids to associate reading and writing with intimacy and security.

Picture Books to Introduce Perspective Writing

I capitalize on the reading/writing connection when sharing text. Sometimes students can use their inferences while reading as a starting point to create new writing.

Patricia MacLachlan's picture book *What You Know First* is the story of a family having to leave the family farm and a young girl's need to memorize what she knows so she won't forget it. It's a good text to model inference in reading. It also serves as an example of illustrations providing or rounding out mental pictures, especially when we don't have the schema to fully comprehend because of the time period, the geography, the culture, and so forth. The following is a list of ways you might use this text.

What You Know First *Repeated Reading Ideas*
* Read initially, generating questions.
* Reread making inferences on the same chart.
* Research the Dust Bowl on the Internet, then read again to see if the book fits the time period.
* Reread using the text for perspective writing—how would the book be different if written by another character?
* Reread to study repeated lines. What is the author's purpose in repeating lines?
* Use for choral reading.

Invariably with this text, the kids are angry that the family is leaving and are upset with the parents. This is where inference comes in, and we begin to discuss what might be behind the move. The black-and-white illustrations help us determine that the story takes place in the past (judging by the cars, in the 1930s or 1940s). We talk about the details that lead us to infer that it is not a choice, that this move is being forced upon the family. We discuss the father's sadness, the intimate way he touches and talks to his favorite cow. This isn't a man who is leaving because he wants to; this is a man with no other choice.

I use their anger to push their thinking, to go deeper than their initial evaluation of the text; this encourages them to think, stimulates rich discussion, and reinforces that each character has a story to tell. The writing mini-lesson that day might be about perspective.

Using the same format and language as Patricia MacLachlan, we might rewrite the story from another character's point of view. Together, we talk about what the dad might be thinking, about the shame he may be feeling at losing a farm that had been in the family for generations. We wonder if fear is behind his actions or what he's hiding from the kids to keep the family going and functioning. Then we write about it together, using the book's text to help structure our writing.

We wrote the following piece with students in a sixth-grade class. Kids chimed in as we continued to chart their ideas. We used the same repeating phrase Patricia MacLachlan used in her text—"I couldn't, if I wanted"—with the dad as the main character instead of the young girl.

Papa
I couldn't
If I wanted
Tell my wife and kids
That we needed to go,
Had to go.
Couldn't tear them from
the house we knew
the places we've been,
the land we know so well.

I couldn't tell them
Or make them feel,
The history we have here,
The connection to the land.

How do you show someone
The memories tucked away,
Have them hear the conversations
So fresh on my mind,
Yet so old.

I remember mama, standing there
Gazing across the prairie,
Tears in her eyes
The beauty too much to bear.

How do I have them feel
The wood planks the same way
My father did as he lovingly
Built the barn,
Beam by beam, that look in his eyes.

How can I tell them about
Love for relatives, for blood,
For relationships built on
History, that nothing else matters.

I couldn't, if I wanted to,
Show them the pain, the sadness,
The failure I feel at having lost
All of this.

I had to, didn't want to,
Sell it all off.
Pack memories away,
And put lives on hold.

Picture books can show how authors write about familiar topics and experiences in new ways; their language, rhythms, and perspectives show us common events in an uncommon light. This fall I tried this technique while on the Pine Ridge Indian Reservation in South Dakota. On vacation, I consult for Cornerstone, a National Literacy Reform Initiative at the University of Pennsylvania in Philadelphia. This project, under Ellin Keene's direction, seeks to improve literacy instruction to our nation's poorest kids in the poorest districts. One of the districts I work with is Shannon County Schools in South Dakota, located on the Pine Ridge Indian Reservation.

On the Pine Ridge Indian Reservation in South Dakota, I observed one seventh-grade teacher modeling this technique using Cynthia Rylant's book *Night in the Country*. She read the text and then related her experience of the previous evening, her own "night in the country": She was in the barn feeding the horses and heard a mountain lion scream nearby. She talked of her fear, of feeling trapped even though the barn was only about a hundred feet from the house. On that night, though, that hundred feet felt like a hundred miles. She recounted how her heart raced and for a moment, she stood paralyzed in fear. She wanted to run and pull the door shut, but momentarily was frozen.

This was high-interest stuff, and it evoked a lot of similar stories from her seventh graders. They sat in silence while she read, then they erupted with energy. They rushed to tell their stories of similar experiences, of times in the Badlands when they had heard animal screams, the lonely howl of coyotes, the snarl of bobcats.

The kids flocked back to their desks and began to write. Their teacher was shocked. She had struggled to get this tough class to write. Her modeling, though, coupled with a real purpose set them on fire.

The three of us teachers walked around the room and jotted down powerful student writing—words, phrases, sentences. As we conferred with the kids, we sought to explain why their writing was powerful. These kids weren't used to being successful. The demonstration that day changed their view of writing, and our notes about their beautiful way with words validated their writing. Their teacher had begun to turn their attitude from defeat toward success.

Novel Excerpts as Models

Of course, picture books are not the only way to stimulate students' ideas and writing. Some classic pieces from novels should be shared with kids, excerpts that are so good, so beautifully written that they should be imprinted on their hearts. One powerful excerpt is the first chapter of *Holes* by Louis Sachar. It's evocative and earthy, with a twist of wit.

> *Here's a good rule to remember about rattlesnakes and scorpions: If you don't bother them, they won't bother you.*
>
> *Usually.*
>
> *Being bitten by a scorpion or even a rattlesnake is not the worst thing that can happen to you. You won't die.*
>
> *Usually.*
>
> *Sometimes a camper will try to be bitten by a scorpion, or even a small rattlesnake. Then he will get to spend a day or two recovering in his tent, instead of having to dig a hole out on the lake.*
>
> *But you don't want to be bitten by a yellow-spotted lizard. That's the worst thing that can happen to you. You will die a slow and painful death.*
>
> *Always.*
>
> *If you get bitten by a yellow-spotted lizard, you might as well go into the shade of the oak trees and lie in the hammock.*
>
> *There is nothing anyone can do for you anymore.*
>
> Sachar, *Holes* (2000, p. 1)

After we study Sachar's writing, we try to mimic his style. We try to build the same anticipation of something by using a pattern of repeated phrases. Then, just as the audience catches on to a pattern set by repeated words (like Sachar's "usually"), we slip them a zinger like, "Always. There is nothing anyone can do for you anymore." Right when it looks like the pattern is predictable, it's disrupted by the opposite comment.

Another great book is *Tuck Everlasting*, whose first chapter resonates with the same passion as Harper Lee's *To Kill a Mockingbird*. The writing is brilliant. Natalie Babbitt sets up the entire book with a lead that is very clear, yet leaves you curious.

> *The first week of August hangs at the very top of the summer, the top of the live-long year, like the seat of a Ferris wheel when it pauses in its turning. The weeks that come before are only a climb from the balmy spring, and those that follow a drop to the chill of autumn, but the first week of August is motionless, and hot. It is curiously silent, too, with bland white dawns and glaring noons, and sunsets smeared with too much color. Often at night there is lightning, but it quivers all alone. There is no thunder, no relieving rain. These are strange and breathless days, the dog days, when people are led to do things they are sure to be sorry for after.*
>
> Babbitt, *Tuck Everlasting* (1986, p. 3)

What compelling writing! What an apt description of stifling Midwestern summers. She baits us so we have to read on to find out what things "they are sure to be sorry for after." Later in the chapter, Babbitt catches us off guard with the casual-seeming line, "As she did once every ten years, to meet her two sons, Miles and Jesse." Every *ten* years?! Every ten years whether she needed it or not?

And Winnie. Babbitt doesn't say that Winnie decided to run away. She decided to "think" about running away, as if it were a huge step to even consider the notion. Babbitt divulges a great deal about Winnie in that simple statement.

After we read an excerpt like this, we experiment with details. We look at words in a different way, and we want to see if we can use the same techniques. The techniques of mentor writers may be difficult to mimic, but the mere engagement with the text enriches us as writers.

We are surrounded with incredible tween text that cries out for us to bring it into the classroom. There is a wealth of interesting material to explore with tweens, to figure out what the authors are doing and how and why. For example, Jerry Spinelli, in *Stargirl*, plays with us and teases us:

> *"Did you see her?"*

Four words is all it takes to set you immediately wondering who "she" is. He strings us along:

> *"Did you see her?"*
>   *That was the first thing Kevin said to me on the first day of school, eleventh grade. We were waiting for the bell to ring.*
>   *"See who?" I said.*
>   *"Hah!" He craned his neck, scanning the mob. He had witnessed something remarkable; it showed on his face. He grinned, still scanning. "You'll know."*
>   Spinelli, *Stargirl* (2002, p. 3)

Look how Spinelli piques our curiosity. Look how he has Kevin scanning the crowd for her, scanning the crowd for a person he hasn't met yet, which makes us want to meet her even more. Then, when he says, "You'll know," he tells us that it will be obvious, but we want to know how we'll know.

The beauty of such writing is that it's short, sweet, and to the point. We can look at a small excerpt and sink our writers' teeth into it.

We are surrounded with amazing lines of text to read aloud, read again, and savor as writers. Repeated lines like those in *Walk Two Moons* by Sharon Creech when the grandfather reflects, "It ain't my marriage bed, but it'll have to do." This simple line gives us a window into the relationship of the grandfather and his beloved Gooseberry, and is repeated throughout the novel.

We use this line to kick off a study of repeated phrases—the way an author will use a repeated phrase to bring us back to the purpose of the writing. We also look at other texts and other picture books to study this technique. Then we try to write in the same way.

In *Baby* Patricia MacLachlan writes about a grieving family blessed with a baby left on the doorstep. She almost puts us in the baby's mind by writing of the baby's memories in snippets, giving us little memories in little phrases. Then she follows these with the actual events that precipitated the memory.

> *She remembered the color red: red flowers that bloomed in winter, cold red sunsets, and especially a tiny teardrop of red that glowed like fire in the light. She now wore it around her neck, but when she thought of it she could remember the feel of it in her hand, how her fingers curled*

around it. Sometimes she opened her hand, expecting to see it there shining in the pocket of her palm.

Red always made her happy.

MacLachlan, *Baby* (1995, p. 64)

Andrew Clements is an author whose books resonate with tweens because the characters and events are so real. This guy knows kids and knows schools. It's obvious that he is a teacher.

It's after the shower. That's when it happens. . . . It's what I see in the mirror. It's what I don't see. I look a second time, and then rub at the mirror again. I'm not there. That's what I'm saying. I'm. Not . . . There.

Clements, *Things Not Seen* (2004, p. 1)

Students love these lines because they are so dramatic and begin the book with an air of mystery that draws the kids to read on. This passage easily kicks off a writing study of leads.

❋ ❋ ❋

These authors provide the "perfect" models and can be mentors for our kids in ways that we can't all be. Like apprentices, we study, dissect, and examine what the masters produce. As apprentices, we observe, listen, practice, make mistakes, ask questions, then practice some more, all the while knowing that approximations are a necessary step in the process. Through these approximations we learn and grow.

Gradually, the apprentices produce work that looks, feels, and sounds more and more like that of the masters. As a community of apprentice writers, immersed in and surrounded by the masters, we have infinite opportunities for growth, for improvement, and for success.

7

Jump-Starting Quality Standards

A few colleagues sat together at the end of a long day, frustrated, tired, beaten, commiserating about the plight of teachers today; in other words, another normal day! It was a familiar conversation, one we had each year as we grew more and more desperate. It was the conversation about "kids coming in lower and lower," compounded by larger class size. Our jobs are harder now than they've ever been. We have a dynamic team of teachers, and we aren't a group of whiners. Our frustrations were the result of our unsuccessful attempts to create skilled writers and readers.

The writing quality in my third/fourth-grade classroom that year was probably the lowest I'd ever experienced. The writing was so poor that I couldn't read their work; the kids had to read it to me. There was no way I could take work home, no way I could assess writing if they weren't in the room because it was unintelligible. Even more pathetic, when I sat and had them read their writing to me, they were often unable to read their own work. Until that day in the lounge, I thought it was just my classroom. It wasn't just my room; it was all our fourth-grade classrooms.

It is important to accept students where they are and take them where they need to go. Therefore, we accepted their writing performance, even though it was so awful. Part of that acceptance of substandard work was probably a result of not wanting to shame our kids who performed poorly. As Carol Lyons, in *Teaching Struggling Readers: How to Use Brain-Based Research to Maximize Learning*, writes:

> Continued emotional distress can create deficits in a child's intellectual abilities, crippling the capacity to learn. That is why it is so important to look for and support the child's approximations or partially right responding and show him how to complete the processing. Without the will to learn, the child will not learn to read and write. (2003, p. 68)

Yet what we were doing in writing was not working when it came to our students' performances on state tests, and to continue was a recipe for disaster. We needed to step out of our comfort zone and try some new things. We had nothing to lose and a lot to gain.

Instead of complaining and accepting our plight, we began to talk, to question, and to stretch our own thinking. Why were we accepting quality like this from kids we believed were extremely intelligent? Why were we working harder than they were? Why were our suggestions in writing conferences unheeded and our teaching points ignored? Why were we still nagging kids in fourth grade about which side of the paper the holes go on and about capital letters for proper names? How could we raise the standards and produce writers who could write, communicate, and touch audiences?

We continued our conversation on an early-release day and then delved deeper into the ramifications of our dilemma. We soon realized there were socioeconomic and philosophical implications to our dilemma. Other schools in our district are more affluent and continually score among the highest on the state's standardized tests. Our school consistently scored at the bottom. Not close to the bottom. The bottom.

Our students are bright, fun, and wonderful kids. None of us believed our kids were less intelligent than the kids in the high-performing schools. We began to wonder if our colleagues in the affluent schools would accept the same quality of work we accepted as the norm. Would those teachers accept papers without end punctuation marks, with incorrect capitalization, lack of consistent thought, or incomplete answers? We began to wonder if our acceptance of the poor writing quality was a pronouncement of socioeconomic predictions. Were we unwittingly dumbing down expectations for our students and establishing what they *wouldn't* achieve?

If we truly believed our students were as intelligent and capable as our more affluent neighbors, did our actions correlate with this belief? We realized that they didn't. We all believed that we had high expectations for our students, yet our practices didn't match our beliefs. Our acceptance of substandard work was proof that we didn't expect as much from lower socioeconomic students. Our actions supported the notion that we should have different standards for poorer kids. We were shocked.

The party was over. We needed to raise consciousness about the need for quality standards as quickly as possible. We needed a pep rally to draw attention to the writing quality, to create a wave of excitement for quality improvement while we worked for longer-term solutions to the situation. Our fourth-grade team became a "School Pep Band," and it was time for a rousing refrain of "Sweet Georgia Brown"!

We decided to address directly and publicly a community concern that we favored writing process at the expense of correct writing conventions. As our kids saw improvement in their quality, we hoped it would change their perceptions about their writing capacity and capabilities. We believe that students love challenges and love to compete with themselves, and in that challenge, they create a view of themselves as capable students because they are successful.

More important, though, we wanted a very public, visible display that we supported high expectations in writing conventions, that proper conventions were a priority for us. In the process, we hoped it would boost our performance on the state tests without lots of test preparation. It's not fun always being on the bottom.

Raising the Standards

We decided to start with a quick hit—a massive push for quality improvement in a short time. We identified our focus areas for the following three to six weeks. The list seemed so basic, so obvious:

* Indent new paragraphs.
* Obey margins.
* Keep the margins straight instead of every line angling down the page.

* Spell basic words correctly.
* Closer approximations of harder words. If we couldn't easily read the word, it was unacceptable.
* Write legibly. If handwriting was not decipherable, it was unacceptable.
* Space words well.

We wanted a big event to get kids revved up and ready to work. All fourth-grade students were pulled into the library to kick off the program in a massive show of unity. We had huge signs made for the classrooms that said, "The Party Is Over." It was a show of force. We outlined the program, why we were doing it, what it would mean to them. We posted the provisions of the program in every room.

We enlisted the support of our specials team (Physical Education, Computer, Art), the principal, the assistant principal, our para-professionals, and Title I and Special Education teachers so we were consistent and unified. We wanted the kids to know we were united in our expectations of higher-quality work. We wanted the students to know these issues were vital to their writing, to their ability to communicate, to self-esteem that comes from producing good quality work, and to being a high-functioning student. We all stood in agreement about the importance of improving quality.

We soon realized we had made a glaring error in compiling this list. Our overall goal was to produce writers who could write clearly, using proper conventions to make the intent of the writing clear. We had listed only conventions of print. This sent the wrong message to our students—that conventions were the indicator of good writing, that content and the message had nothing to do with it. We had initially believed that we would focus our assessment on conventions alone, but we soon realized that focus was too narrow. We quickly expanded the list to include ideas, organization, and complete thoughts.

Modeling for the New Standards

We set aside three weeks in which we would model these conventions in whole-class crafting lessons while writing with the students. Our Title I and Special Education colleagues did the same, modeling what these standards looked like, working with the students to affect change in their writing. We wrote deeply about various topics in our modeling for students, making note of writing conventions, explicitly demonstrating why the conventions were essential.

As we modeled our writing in front of our classes, we were demonstrating what good writers do in the writing process. A writing demonstration sounded something like this:

Today, I'm still working on my piece about my bicycle trip through Canada. If you remember, yesterday I was writing about how we had reached the point, after one thousand miles on a bike seat in the shadows of the incredible Canadian Rocky Mountains, we came around a corner and said, "Oh, look, another beautiful mountain." There was no excitement, no energy, no real appreciation of the beauty; we just wanted off those bike seats! As you know, I've been working on my writing plan for the last two days. That plan guides my writing and allows me to focus on how I'm writing, not on what I'm going to write. I'm at the place in my plan where I'm writing about the beauty.

> *The bright morning light threw shadows onto the pavement below.*
>
> *Wherever we went, whether we were sailing and screaming down hills hanging on for dear life or puffing up steep grades, we were surrounded by mountains. Not just any mountains . . . tall, magestic, rugged mountains.*

When I began a new paragraph, I moved the writing over about 5 spaces, or about the size of my thumb. I do that to tell the audience that something new has happened. It's called indenting and it's a cue to the readers; it helps their comprehension. Last week we spent every day on the need for capital letters. I used capital letters on Canada *and the* Canadian Rockies *because they are names of places. I am not sure if* magestic *is spelled correctly, but I don't want to stop now because it will stop my flow of writing, so I'll circle it and come back to it later.*

> *I knew I should be appreciating the beauty of those peaks, and I had for weeks. Now, though, I would appresiate nothing more than a comfortable car seat and a vehicle that would go faster than ten mph! I wanted off of that seat in the worst way.*

I circled appresiate *because I know it's spelled incorrectly but don't want to interrupt the flow of my writing to look it up. I want you to focus on my new paragraph. Again, I moved the words in 5 spaces.*

Writers indent the first line of a new paragraph to tell the reader that something has changed. Turn to your partner and discuss why I began a new paragraph. What change did I want you to be aware of with a new paragraph?

We all continued these writing demonstrations for three weeks. We began focusing on one skill at a time, then we built on those skills with each week. First, we demonstrated capital letters, then moved on to paragraphs. After the demonstrations, kids went back to their desks for their own composing time. In our conferences, we focused on the skills we had demonstrated that day. We took anecdotal notes of which kids were correctly using the convention and which kids needed more help (to be given in invitational groups). We made notes about which conventions they were consistently using and what their next steps would be.

Writing Prompts with a Purpose

To monitor student growth, our fourth-grade team decided to give a consistent writing prompt to every fourth grader once every three weeks. We chose the three-week cycle because we felt strongly that self-selected topics are an essential part of the writing program, so we were leery of too many prompts.

Every three weeks the students had two days to write to a prompt. We tried to select prompts that were suitable to our students' knowledge and experience. We wanted the prompts to be as realistic as possible and applicable to as many students as possible. The prompts included:

* Write about a memorable day in your life and tell why it was memorable.
* Write about a lesson you learned in life. What was the lesson and how did you learn that lesson?
* Write about a person you admire and why. What attributes does that person have that make you admire him or her?
* Describe an event or obstacle that prevented you from achieving something. What was that obstacle and how did you overcome it?

We chose the two-day writing model to mirror our state testing format. We felt it would be an easy way to replicate the state testing situation without compromising our writing instruction. We allowed each student two separate class periods of fifty minutes each. The first day was for planning and completion of a first draft; the second day was for revisions, editing, and production of a final copy. There were no teacher conferences or editing. No peer conferences. No talking. Each student was on his or her own.

We made two exceptions to state testing guidelines. State testing does not allow use of dictionaries or other spelling tools. We value the ability to access resources to help with writing, so we expect kids to use their spelling dictionaries, word walls, and environmental print to edit their spelling. We allowed our kids to use all of them when editing.

State testing also allows no oral planning before the kids write. We didn't agree with this either, so we spent a lot of time planning orally before having the kids write. In whole-class planning sessions, we brainstormed ideas about what they could write about. We wanted the kids to have time to verbalize ideas and get ideas from others that might spark something in their own writing. We placed a priority on planning before putting the pencil to paper.

At the end of the two days, we traded student writing with another fourth-grade teacher. This allowed us to be more objective. We also did this to establish a sense of urgency on the part of the students, to raise expectations because the writing was being assessed by another teacher, and to keep a sense, as in state testing, that the papers would be evaluated by someone who didn't know the writer intimately. For ourselves, we wanted a look at the writing quality in the other classrooms to see if we were keeping our expectations high enough.

We scored the papers using ideas from the Six Trait writing assessment tool from the Northern Regional Educational Lab (Culham 2003). To keep our efforts manageable, we limited the assessment to three areas: conventions, ideas, and organization. We evaluated each area according to the following rubric:

5 = Strong. Shows control of the writing process.
4 = Effective. The strengths outweigh the negatives, very little revision is needed.
3 = Developing. Strengths and weaknesses fairly equal.
2 = Emerging. The negatives outweigh the strengths.
1 = Not There Yet. Lots of issues need work; no control of the writing.

With the first prompt, we all had many incredible papers that were thoughtful and interesting and were well organized with an obvious purpose, but they had substandard conventions. Other papers had no purpose, made no sense, and had no obvious ending, but they had stellar capitalization, punctuation marks, and spelling. It appeared that these students believed that conventions alone were the sign of good writing. Wrong!

We realized an added benefit of trading papers—the opportunity to compare the writing in our classrooms. This revealed writing trends across the classrooms.

We began to include our observations of overall student assessment when we returned the papers. We used those observations in subsequent teaching lessons. Now, in addition to his or her own observations, a teacher could say to the class, "If you remember, Mrs. Ziegler commented that we need to continue to work on making our purpose more clear." Such comments from another fourth-grade teacher could be used in whole-class learning experiences, for example, while modeling with picture books or writing along with the class.

Special Education and the Standards

Our team had many spirited discussions about our special education kids. We wanted to make the experience challenging enough to push their limits while not making the standard inaccessible to them. At the same time, we all felt that we tended to underestimate the abilities of our kids, and didn't necessarily know what our special ed kids could attain. We talked among ourselves about the backgrounds of those kids and where they had grown and we compared initial writing assessments to see what was reasonable while not limiting growth.

Learning is harder for some kids, and that is just the way it is. There's no reason to mask that. Some people have to work harder to learn, and will always have to.

I am blunt with kids. Many times I just say, "You know, buddy, you're a smart, smart ticket, just like I am. For people like us, sometimes we have to work harder than some people. But, we get there. It may take us longer, but we always get there, and we can feel better about it because we did the hard work to get there."

The quality of writing in our classrooms quickly improved as a result of a common focus on a few standards. Kids became more aware of the conventions necessary to communicate in writing. Only three kids in my room met minimal expectations after the first prompt. After the second prompt, fifteen students made it, a huge jump. Huge progress in a short time.

As quickly as overall writing improved, the separation between the kids who could do the required work and those who couldn't was obvious. The kids who weren't taking the time and the care to demonstrate quality conventions were totally different from the ones who didn't have the skills to produce high-quality work. Of course, we want all our kids to meet the standard eventually. The kids who struggle have experienced a lot of failure and are afraid that failure is really who they are. Brian Cambourne (1993) reassures us that kids will engage in the task at hand if they feel they can be successful. It's our job to break the learning into small enough steps that they can feel success.

We're Smarter Than We Thought

One night not long after we started working together with common prompts, I was wide awake at 4:00 AM with a brainstorm. It was one of those realizations that get you up and out of bed. I shuffled downstairs and pulled out their writing samples to check out my hunch. I averaged the scores my kids had received in all three areas we assessed. The average score in Ideas and Content was 2.6 on a 5-point scale. The average score in Organization was 2.5. The average Conventions score was a dismal 1.5. That was the information I needed.

The next morning before the kids came in, I made charts listing the results of the first sample. I posted them on the back wall and pulled the kids together in the front of the room. That day I began with this question: "Of the three traits assessed, which is the hardest?" They all agreed it was getting ideas together and assembling what they were going to write about. They all felt Organization was next hardest. How they structured the information posed a great deal of problems. Conventions were the easiest for them.

I had the classroom turn around to view the results. They were shocked that the hardest things had earned them the highest scores and that the easiest trait had yielded the lowest scores. For the next few weeks, I repeatedly reinforced, "Look at our average. We simply *must* address our spelling, paragraph, and capital letter issues to get those scores up."

The pathetic showing on the first sample was a rallying point, a call to action. When we started the second prompt, the classroom felt different. The kids were more focused, more intent. They used the entire time given instead of being finished in twenty minutes. I walked around the room, making notes of who was doing a great job and who was shutting down. I pulled the kids who were overwhelmed for a pep talk, letting them know I believed in them, that they could do it.

As I walked around, I watched as Jack labored over his piece. He had never produced more than he did that morning. Jack had started the year reading at the pre-primer level and his writing, when he wrote, was indecipherable. He used to feel proud when he managed to write a sentence. That day, as he filled the page, he took out his Quick Word and began to correct his spelling. He added details and corrected capital letters. This kid was motivated. When I called "time," I sent him to the principal's office with his latest work to show off. He beamed with pride. I took him to the phone to call home and relay the great news.

***

Writing conventions are a small part of communicating with an audience. Without proper conventions of print, however, a powerful message can be lost somewhere between writer and reader. Our students are learning that it is the writer's job to communicate so that the audience can understand the writing.

However, expanding our assessment to include ideas and organization was the key to creating better writers. Providing feedback to students about their progress and using the assessment to drive instruction helped raise our fourth-grade standardized test scores.

8

Writing Beyond Narrative: Genre Studies

uring state testing one of my gifted fourth-grade writers sat staring off into space for almost half of the first hour, writing nothing. Finally, unable to contain myself, I went over and hissed, "What are you doing, Breanna?" Full of disdain, she announced, "I don't like this prompt. I'm not going to write because it doesn't fit me as a writer." I had duped the students into thinking that all writing should be self-selected.

Breanna's reaction to the writing prompt indicated that I needed to offer a well-rounded curriculum that included various genre studies in brief time periods so that students are exposed to a wide range of reading and writing experiences throughout the year. The more kids read and write in various genres, and understand those genres, the more flexible they will be. The more contact and exposure students have to different genres, the more familiar they will be with that genre, and be able to embrace other genres. And the more we study text features and characteristics of different genres, the better thinkers kids will be, and that's the end goal.

Unfortunately, some of us teachers let our preferences and strong suits get the better of us. We spend more time on teaching what we like and what we are comfortable with. For example, I am the personal narrative, realistic fiction king. It's my favorite genre. I love reading it, love writing it, and love to model using personal narrative texts. When I go to the bookstore, I head right for New Fiction. I hate fantasy. Hate it, pure and simple. Science fiction is the same. I just don't like it, feel nothing for it, and have always muscled my way through it when required.

Some kids hate personal narrative as much as I hate science fiction and fantasy. I decided I owed it to my kids to branch out into different genres, and the experience was humbling. Last year I decided to dabble in fantasy, so I began the planning and immersion. I did a great job bringing fantasy novels into the classroom and had a good time modeling reading strategies using fantasy short stories, but then it came time to model fantasy writing. What a nightmare. For the first time in years, I dreaded writing time because I had to write and it was horrible.

I always preach that it's important to live the writer's life so I know the struggles that my writers go through, but this was ridiculous. Every day, when I called the kids to the Oval Office, they'd drag up to the front to watch me struggle and wrestle with this genre. I felt like I did at my first Junior/Senior Prom when Patti Myers looked over at me and asked, "Wanna French?" I couldn't get out of that '65 Ford Galaxie fast enough, and I couldn't get out of the fantasy writing situation any quicker.

I was trying to write this cute, funny fantasy piece about the kids in our classroom, only it was in the future. Having them be the star characters, grown up and living adult lives, would be a sure-fire way to keep them engaged. It was dismal. There was no life in the classroom, no energy in the demonstrations, and no push on my part to spend time writing.

One day, after watching the kids drag to the front for the next demonstration of my fantasy writing in progress, I finally asked what was going on. As usual, they were blunt. They told me in short order. "Your writing stinks," Jordan replied. Ahhh, the joy of teaching.

"Oh, is that right?" I said, getting defensive. I looked over at my colleague who was observing. Her head was down on the table, her shoulders shaking with laughter. Finally I began to laugh too. "It does stink, doesn't it?"

"Duhhhh," John whispered. The tension lifted, and the kids began to openly make fun of my writing. They were merciless, but in their teasing responses, they brought back the energy and fun that is usually part of the writer's block. They were so honest with me about my writing at that moment that it opened them to take risks in their writing in the future. On another day, Eli was struggling with his own fantasy. I was empathizing with him until he said, "It's bad, but not as bad as yours."

For the remainder of the year, my fantasy writing was a classroom joke. They'd refer to it when they were struggling. Holt, hating the poetry we were working on, looked at me once and said, "Remember that fantasy you wrote? Remember? Yeah . . . well, this is that!" I shook my head. Finally I understood. Instead of using some energizing teacher line to push him to new heights, I said, "Let me help you get through this one. We'll do it together."

Kids can't choose whether to take part in our genre studies. They must take part, must be involved, must read and write in that genre, and must publish. The teacher's attitude, though, changes the nature of the writing; we can't expect every kid to be an expert in every genre. The following list has some genres we often study with tweens because they will encounter these genres often in and out of school.

Biography	Historical Fiction
Textbooks/Reference Text	Persuasion
Realistic Fiction	Poetry
Memoir/Autobiography	Science Fiction
Mystery	Journalism Opinion/Editorial
Tests	Expository Text (Narrative or
Picture Book	Didactic)
Promotional Materials and	Photo Essay
Advertising	Fantasy

Kids who are well versed in text structures of various genres will use the knowledge with reading and writing tasks throughout their lives. The kinds of reading and writing a person does in a day includes all genres: editorials, persuasive writing, nonfiction, manuals for computers, e-mails, summaries, reports, and personal and business letters.

Launching a New Genre Study

I learned what not to do when introducing a genre. On the day I began a study of persuasive writing, some Public Education and Business

Coalition (PEBC) Lab teachers were observing. In the PEBC Lab experience, teachers observe in the classroom for several days in the morning. Then in the afternoon, we debrief.

We gathered in the Oval Office for my demonstration lesson. The music, gym, and computer teachers had been complaining that our class was becoming hard to manage. I decided this would be the perfect chance to introduce persuasive writing to the kids. We would write letters to the specials teachers to ask forgiveness and a second chance.

I whipped off our task at hand and showed the kids charts I had made that listed features of good persuasive text. I went over the rationale behind writing the letter, sure they'd get excited and see the purpose. They didn't. My excitement was met with apathy.

When everyone went to their seats to begin writing, many kids acted out and were messing around. Finally, in frustration, I gathered the visiting teachers together and we stood back to watch. Lane was busy cutting erasers off his pencils. Jack was busily playing around with John and would smile when he'd catch our eyes. Nick and Shawn were eagerly playing with their Bionicals. Only two kids were actively engaged with their writing; the rest were wandering around, playing with paper footballs, waiting in line for the bathroom pass, and generally acting up. The room was loud, not that beautiful kind of loud that comes from talking and working, but loud with fighting and nervousness. I was humiliated.

I pulled the kids into the Oval Office to switch gears to reading. I read orally to settle them back down. I gave instructions for what they were watching for in their text that day and turned them loose. The group quickly settled into their normal routines, and quickly the room had that hum I live for, the quiet talking about good text and the playfulness that comes from kids being immersed with great literature. We teachers stood on the fringe of the room, amazed at the difference.

Later in the debriefing with the visitors, we talked about what had happened, what had gone wrong, why the extreme differences in writing and reading behaviors. I realized that when I began, we hadn't studied persuasive writing in reading so they had no schema for the genre. I listed the text features instead of letting the kids discover what made good persuasive writing. I selected the topic instead of getting the buy-in from self-selected text. The topic was a priority for me, but not for them! I started off too dry and too clinical instead of being playful.

A Fresh Start

I changed plans and was ready for the next day. This time would be better. I scrapped all my beautiful charts and asked the kids about their own schema with persuasiveness. They looked at me blankly. "When have you convinced your parents to let you do something they initially didn't want you to do?" Now they were hooked. They started talking excitedly with each other, laughing and chatting as they gave details. "That is persuasive thinking. Now, what do you do and say when you try to persuade friends to do something they don't want to do?" Again, I charted their comments and posted the charts in the room to refer to later.

I pulled in persuasive text to use during reading that week. Mondo Publishing offers some new books with a similar format and different themes. They are collections of short essays written by tweens around a theme, with contributors arguing for or against the issue; for example, *Should There be Zoos?* and *Should We Have Pets?*

I introduced the books, and immediately the kids reacted with anger and disbelief that anyone their age thought there shouldn't be pets or zoos. I passed out the books and directed them to read with partners, going through the text twice, once for comprehension and once to notice features of persuasive text.

As they read, I circulated around the room conferring with kids, asking what they noticed about persuasive writing. I listed in my notes kids who were getting it and wrote what they told me. During reading response time, I pulled those kids to the front and had them share what they had noticed as I charted their reactions and thoughts.

After several days with the reading, more and more kids were able to identify features of persuasive text, so it was time to make the leap to their own writing, this time with a topic for which every kid had schema. The kids were to work in pairs or individually and their task was to convince their parents that they should give a specific present. Before I sent them to write, we verbally reviewed the process to give as many models as possible. As the kids tried to convince me that they needed the toy, I countered with reasons that they shouldn't get the present. The kids caught on quickly, realizing that to write persuasively, they had to know the arguments against their proposal. We charted these arguments on paper too.

The kids' engagement was proof they were ready to try this. I didn't want them to actually write yet because their thinking about the topic was not solid enough, and I believe in discussing a topic before they write about it. This echoes Katie Wood Ray's thinking that if we spend more time thinking and talking before writing, the first draft will be better and will require less revision.

I had the kids do some role playing, taking on either the role of parent or classmate. The kids were laughing and talking and relating to each other. I walked around, noting great arguments in my teacher reflection book. When the excitement reached its highest pitch, I called the kids back to the Oval Office. (I always stop an activity right when it reaches the crescendo so they'll want more of it. The collective groans and protests of the kids let me know I had engagement!) I noted their thinking and arguments, charting on paper as we talked. By identifying what they were doing well, I was gradually releasing control to them, and this thinking gave many kids more content.

Now the kids were ready to write down their arguments to parents about why they should get the specific toy. They chose partners to write with or wrote individually. They had some leeway within our common topic.

When I begin something new like this, there might be a small group of kids who are still leery and afraid to try the task on their own. We do a shared writing experience. They sit with me and we draft together, combining their ideas into a shared piece. We brainstorm what could be said, and I list their ideas on the chart paper. They are instructed to stay as long as they need, but when ready, they can leave the group and find a friend or write by themselves. When I see they're ready, like a mother robin, I start to nudge them out of the nest.

Again, since this is a new genre, I expect lots of really horrible writing. Expecting it keeps the frustration down; if it's awful, well, it's their first attempt, and it will be better the next time around. The focus is on growth within the genre and the improvement as we continue to write.

Balancing Writing and Reading in Genre Studies

During the first weeks of any genre study we read in that genre, detail characteristics together in crafting lessons, identify text features of the genre, and have repeated demonstrations. The writers have as much time with the genre reading as possible before they try to write in the genre.

Picture books can be helpful in building knowledge about a new genre that we are studying. For two to three weeks we read as many picture books as we can in that genre, study the text features as we chart our observations, and then we attempt to use those text features to write in that genre ourselves. Here's a brief list of possible books:

Title	*Author*	*Strategies*
Historic Fiction Picture Books		
Faithful Elephants	Yukio Tsuchiya	Schema, questioning, synthesis
Terrible Things	Eve Bunting	Questioning, inference, schema
Smoky Nights	Eve Bunting	Questioning, schema
Nonfiction Picture Books		
Hidden Witness	Jackie Napolean Williams	Determining importance, schema
Passage to Freedom: the Sugihara Story	Ken Mochizuki	Schema, inference, questioning
So Far from the Sea	Eve Bunting	Inference, schema

When we study historic fiction, the students select from books about the West and Colorado since our social studies curriculum includes Colorado history. For their guided reading groups, they choose from the following books:

* *Streams to the River, Rivers to the Sea*, a novel by Scott O'Dell about Sacagawea and Lewis and Clark
* *Sing Down the Moon*, another Scott O'Dell novel about Native Americans being moved to reservations
* Books by Kenneth Thomasma: *Naya Nuki, Soun Tetoken,* and *Om-Kas-Toe*, about Native American tribes in the West
* *The Little House on the Prairie* series
* Patricia MacLachlan series, *Sarah Plain and Tall, Skylark,* and *Caleb's Story.*

Reading groups focus on text features of historic fiction. We compile charts listing attributes of good historic fiction and study the author's craft in creating a story. We hypothesize about which events were fiction and which were true or were based on true events.

Good read-aloud books are the Gary Paulsen series, *Mr. Tucket;* it's a five-book series about a young boy separated from his family while traveling across the prairie on a wagon train. As I read orally, I have the class focus on two levels: enjoyment of well-written adventure books and elements of historic fiction. After reading the books and charting what might be true historic events and what might be fiction, we determine that, with my guidance, the books are more realistic fiction than historic fiction. This was a good lesson in the difference between historic and realistic fiction genres.

Historic Fiction

During my reading crafting lessons, we use picture books that are historic fiction to broaden the scope from western historic fiction to general historic fiction.

Writing demonstrations are spent applying what we know about historic fiction to writing we do together as a class. For example, we might write about a real historic event such as the Battle of Glorietta Pass. This Civil War battle took place near the border of New Mexico and Colorado at a high mountain pass. The Confederate Army marched west through Texas and then north to Denver to confiscate the gold reserves there. Colorado, still a territory at that point, got wind of the planned attack and hastily assembled a makeshift army that marched south to intercept the Southern troops before they got to Denver. At Glorietta Pass the two armies engaged. The Southern troops felt safe, surrounded by seemingly impenetrable majestic peaks, and concentrated on the pass between the surrounding peaks.

Many of the Colorado troops were experienced mountain men, used to climbing and scaling sheer precipices. In a surprise attack, the Colorado troops scaled the mountain peaks and came in behind the Confederate troops. Once safely behind the enemy lines, they blew up the Confederate supply wagons and then retreated to safety. The Confederate troops, left without weapons, food, and other necessities, were forced to retreat. Many historians feel that the Civil War would have had drastically different results had the Confederate Troops succeeded in taking the gold from Denver.

This event works well for many reasons. It's high action and drama, which intrigues many of the boys. It happened close to home. The event was also controversial.

John Chivington, an opinionated, gruff, former preacher who laid down the Bible to pick up a gun, led the Colorado troops. After the success at Glorietta Pass, Chivington became a Colorado hero. He also led one of the most brutal, sadistic events in Colorado history when he led troops to a peaceful Cheyenne Indian settlement and slaughtered innocent women and children in the Sand Creek Massacre. The fact that he was a preacher made it all the more horrifying.

We read articles together as I chart details needed to write the historic fiction. Once we have the facts of the battle, we discuss different story lines. Again, I chart the options. We plan for days, exploring different ways we could approach the battle and from different perspectives. Finally, we settle on a story line. Every day, I model using the notes and the planning to write the piece.

We use what we know of Chivington to construct his character, his mannerisms, and his personality. We use people in our own room to create the personalities of the other characters.

We begin the piece in the tent where the Colorado leaders headed by Chivington were planning the attack and the strategy to get behind enemy lines. The writing is high action, which engages the boys. We add lots of gross details about the men being hurt in the climb, which they love. To make sure things don't get too gross, I use the movie rating system to make sure the writing is acceptable; this limits the graphic details since I insist it be a G or PG rating. Writing together takes away the risk for the writers since they can watch and observe, participating as they feel the urge. The writing sessions are interactive, with students chiming in to help determine the plot and its twists and turns. I revise the planning continually as new ideas and events come up.

When the reading and writing demonstration immersion is finished, it is time for the students to start their writing. I always give my writers the option to write about the same event we did together as a class. For writers who were intimidated by the new genre, this provides a sense of safety since the research and writing has already been finished and could serve as a springboard for their writing.

My classes are always heavy with boys. Newkirk (2002) and Smith and Wilhelm (2002) consistently talk about the need to bring technology into the classroom to further engage the boys. Actually, it makes sense to use technology to engage *all* students. While we are doing our research and drafting our pieces about famous Colorado characters, the kids are also spending some time in the computer lab learning how to create a slide show, similar to a PowerPoint presentation. We might spend the next weeks creating slide shows of these Coloradoans. (The first time it took about twice as long as we expected, and it was worth every second.) The class is engaged and excited. We do searches to find photographs of historic people and places.

Finally, we go public. The parents are invited in to school. The kids dress as their characters and present their slide shows.

We continue genre studies throughout the year in this same manner, flip-flopping reading and writing. While we engage in the historic fiction writing, the kids have free choice during reading so they don't become overloaded with too much new information at one time. The genre writing is a big stretch for them so the reading can be more relaxed. We still have guided reading groups, modeling of comprehension strategies, and running records in reading, but in self-selected instead of teacher-selected reading texts. Striving to balance self-selected and teacher-selected texts and topics in reading and writing provides students choices while expanding their repertoire.

Throughout the genre studies, we also integrate skills instruction. For example, if the primary focus is historic fiction, the curriculum might include these items:

* text features of historic fiction,
* use of conflict to engage the audience,
* informing the audience about the intent of the writing,
* correct use of homophones *their, they're,* and *there* (writing prompt observations used here to determine skills to be taught),
* quotation marks for speakers, and
* paragraphs for every new speaker.

As with the introduction of anything new, we use gradual release of control in cycling students through a genre study. Kids who are doing a great job can be brought forward to model their writing. Kids who typically don't get identified as good writers can model their writing as they begin to catch on; sometimes it's only a sentence or paragraph but it's enough so they know they can achieve success too. The more we learn from the study, the more kids have success with the genre, the more excited they will be to try the genre again.

9

Tackling Spelling and Punctuation

I t is a flawless March day in Colorado. The blue skies so blue that it hurts to look at them. There is not a cloud to be found in the sky, not one; not even a wisp. The sunshine is spectacular, glistening on the tender green shoots bursting out and straining for the sun.

Every single inhabitant of the state is outside enjoying the day. Everyone. Senior citizens from the retirement high rise are sitting on the benches outside waving at people, laughing. Kids play in the dirt for the first time all winter. Every human is outside . . . except me. I'm inside doing spelling and punctuation research.

Every two hours, if I've been good, the spelling warden comes in to give me a two-minute break. I get to go the bathroom and gaze out the window at Mt. Evans, splendid in the distance. The snow encrusted peak beckons to all to come and explore. And they do. Thousands of Denver citizens are there now, snowshoeing, skiing, walking. I'm at home doing my research.

Friends stop by and sit in the waiting room for their turn to talk. The warden gives me three minutes for visitation. I walk in, take my seat on the opposite side of the observation glass. My friends take the microphone and whisper, "You're so dedicated, so giving . . ."

"I know," I murmur, "It's just who I am. I am more than happy to sacrifice my own life to teach spelling and punctuation. Somebody has to do it. It might just as well be me." The warden clears his throat, signaling the end of the visit. I put my hand to the glass, a single tear sliding down my cheek before I can catch it.

I read my friend's lips as I shuffle out, "We love you, Bruce. Keep up the good fight!" I wander back to my computer to compile more research.

Back in the cell, I turn on the TV to catch the weather report. A cardboard cutout of the weatherman sits on the desk with a sign that says, "I'm outside enjoying this beautiful day. Tune into our evening broadcast to hear about just how beautiful the day was."

I live in a Victorian home fifteen blocks from the state Capitol building in downtown Denver. My work today has been the equivalent of replacing the float in the tank of a toilet. The float allows the toilet tank to fill up with water and then shut off when full.

I didn't spend the day stripping varnish from the ornate cherry fireplace. I didn't toil all day to put splashes of color on the walls that pick up the colors in the carpet. I didn't replace a 1950s-style chandelier with a classic Victorian reproduction, making the room feel like a vintage place from the past. I spent the day replacing the toilet float.

When my friends come over for a party, nobody will say, "I love what you've done to your toilet float." *Trading Spaces* fans will not pull me into a corner to whisper, "You just have an eye for toilet floats, could you please come and help me with mine?" There will be nobody pulling me to the side in confidence asking, "What did you do to your toilet to make it work so smoothly and effortlessly?"

Nobody will even notice that I worked on the float because it makes no difference to anybody. When it works correctly, nobody even knows that it's working, nobody knows that it is there. When it is working, nobody will even stop to ask, "I wonder what components are inside that toilet that allow it to flush for me?"

But let me tell you, if it's not working, everybody notices, and everybody is mad. Lines will form and people will get cranky. People will have to take the lid off the tank and fish around in the water to pull the handle up manually, and will then have to support the arm with something to keep the arm from returning to the bottom. It's a hassle when it doesn't work, and stops important other work from being done.

Spelling and punctuation are like housework. It's not glamorous, it's not exciting, it's not dramatic. It's just essential. Nobody notices when it's done because when the house looks neat and lovely, it's pleasant to be there and it's easy to move through it. But it's immediately obvious when housework is neglected. Likewise, nobody notices when a writer spells or punctuates correctly, but when they don't, look out. Incorrect spelling and sloppy punctuation prevent a reader from understanding the text. They slow down the process and require that the reader spend an inordinate amount of time deciphering the writing.

Spelling Improvement

Most teaching is constantly evolving. Many teachers vigilantly monitor their classroom practices and revise them as often as necessary. In the busy scheme of things, though, something always get neglected, or at least it doesn't get quite as much attention as it should. Spelling and punctuation are two areas of instruction that are easy to let slide. They just don't seem as important as all the other things we need to teach.

Spelling is a small part of the writing program but it is essential. Spelling is important. When parents ask how their kids are doing in writing, they're not asking if their child has created the next Pulitzer Prize–winning essay. They're asking if they can spell, write neatly, and use correct conventions. Readers judge the intelligence of a writer by the spelling and conventions, and they dismiss writing that is full of spelling errors and has misused or missing punctuation marks. When that happens, any effort that was put into the writing was in vain; any intended message is lost.

The core of a good spelling program is reading. A lot of reading—as much as can be crammed into the day. Kids who read, especially those who read voraciously, tend to be the best spellers. As students improve in reading, their spelling improves as well, even without a formal spelling program. It's the struggling spellers who need more help because they don't pick up on the subtle cues other readers pick up on and use. The teacher has to point out what they miss and try to teach them how to recognize it themselves.

Teacher Demonstration

As I model writing for students, I base the demonstrations on two levels: deep and surface. The deep level is the meaning of the piece, what is said, how it's said, and the message that the writer wants the reader to walk away with. The surface level deals with the mechanics of the language that aid the reader in getting the message.

During a demonstration, regardless of the deep-level focus (genre, strategy, etc.), I also model the conventions of language. As I construct meaning, I point out the spelling strategies I use, reviewing spelling strategies we have studied as a class. For example:

> Today, I am continuing my piece about Lucky getting out of the fish tank and almost dying. If you remember, yesterday I wrote about how I had filled the tank up too high and he must have hopped out. I was at the point where we walked into the room and Tanner yelled that the frog was out.
>
>> We stormed up the ramp and into the mobile, ready to start another day. I was busily collecting field-trip permission slips and taking attendance when Tanner yelled, "The frog is out! The frog is out!" The class rushed over to see what he was talking about.
>>
>> "Oh great," I mumbled. "I must have filled the tank above the line last night. Man, I hope he isn't dead."
>>
>> "He's dead. He's really dead," Taylor yelled, running back to her seat. My stomach lerchd as I ran to Tanner.
>>
>> "Gross," Ian moaned. "He's all red . . ."
>
> Look what I did as an author. I'm following my plan on the chart paper, which allows me to write quickly. Look at the way I spelled above here. If you remember, one of the spelling rules we can count on is that words in English never end in v so I added the e at the end.
>
> Also note that I wanted a powerful word to describe how my stomach felt when I heard Lucky was dead. I wanted a word that would let you know that my stomach was tied in knots, that immediately I was worried and filled with dread. I am not sure if lerchd is spelled right, but it doesn't look right. So, for now, I want to continue writing and I'll look it up later. Say the word with me as I break it into phonemes: ler-ch-d. It's a close approximation, and close enough that I'll remember what it said. I'll circle it so I remember to come back to it, and continue writing.

My demonstration focuses on the meaning I'm making and my physical reaction to Lucky's getting out. At the same time, I am pointing out specific spelling strategies and reinforcing the value of spelling approximations.

Invented Spelling and Approximation

We have struggled with the idea of invented spelling as a school. We feel that we have accepted invented spelling for too long, which has created poor spellers. We still have fourth graders who can't spell basic words such as *they* and *because*.

However, Cambourne (1993) states, "Without the opportunity to approximate, the whole, smooth-running learning cycle is stopped and progress and/or refinement becomes impossible" (p. 69). Learners can't progress without approximation, if they are playing it safe instead of learning new strategies.

Cambourne also believes the role of approximation in learning is the easiest thing for teachers to understand but the hardest thing to put into practice because of the fear that errors will become ingrained in students' knowledge. "There is a very strong consensus in our culture about correctness and error avoidance. Most teachers and parents—in fact, almost everyone who might be included in the 'general public'—have a strong conviction that an integral part of learning is the rooting out of an error before it becomes too firmly established" (p. 67).

Gentry (1989) agrees: "One of the greatest difficulties a child can face in learning to spell is being inhibited from inventing spelling because of the risk of being wrong. Making errors is as natural for learning to spell as 'ditching' is for learning to ride a bike. In both instances, learning cannot take place without error. Not only should spelling errors be tolerated, they should be expected" (p. 9).

We need to encourage invented spelling and approximations. At the same time, we must teach the correct forms of words in manageable lists and studies. Word lists should be made up of basic words that are commonly misspelled in writing. These lists are used to increase the amount of correct spelling and reduce the numbers of times basic words are repeatedly spelled incorrectly in student writing.

Have a Go

A useful procedure that balances approximations with correct spelling is called "Have a Go." Incorrect words are identified and then students have a second chance to attempt to spell the word. It is remarkable how many times the word is corrected on the second try. This is especially useful for tweens, who are often nearing the correct spelling of many words.

In *Spelling Inquiry* (Chandler and Mapleton Teacher-Research Group 1999), the teachers talk about making the students more responsible for their own spelling. "We didn't want to replace the basal spelling series with a teacher-generated 'bag of tricks'; instead, we hoped to develop responsive instructional plans that kept spelling in its proper place in the writing process while ensuring that all students received the assistance—direct and indirect—they need to become conventional spellers."

One way to give control of the writing process to the students is to have them identify how much of the misspelled word they have correct. Many misspellings are close to conventional spellings. Students need only a small amount of scaffolding to be at the correct state, and the majority of the time, the student is able to correct the word.

Multiple Drafts

Emphasis on spelling in a first draft can inhibit the writing. The goal of a first draft is to get ideas on paper, not to spell every word correctly. We need to model ways to be aware of spelling in a first draft while not emphasizing it to the point that it blocks expression of meaning.

Students need support for spelling attempts. Teachers need to validate spelling growth in their writing by noting when improvements have been made. If kids know the teacher supports their attempts, they will be more likely to engage in spelling.

Proofreading is a major component of a good spelling program. As students write, part of the proofreading/editing process is the identification of misspelled words. It is a major step when students can correctly identify misspelled words. It signals that they are conscious of the correct spelling of the word and know that their spelling does not match it.

Circling misspelled words is a step. The students can verify the spelling of circled words later when they have time to proofread and edit. The writing process isn't inhibited because they are approximating words as closely as they can while they continue the writing process.

Some principles for dealing with spelling are:

* Write multiple drafts to encourage risk taking.
* Encourage approximations.

* Have kids pronounce a word slowly and write what they hear.
* Have kids circle suspicious words and continue writing.
* Encourage use of Quick Word Dictionary to find misspelled words.
* Share correction with students.

Spelling Tools

We encourage the use of various spelling tools so that students can be as independent with spelling as possible. Every student has a Quick Word, a spelling dictionary that lists only proper spelling. These inexpensive and easy-to-use tools are vital to students' self-correction. Words are listed alphabetically on a portion of the page, and the remainder of the page is lined for words that aren't given. When kids encounter words in their writing that aren't in the Quick Word, they add them alphabetically. This way, they have a running account of words they can use. The Quick Word also has a section on homophones. Each homophone is listed with a sentence showing it in context.

The kids always want to use Spell Checkers, but it's more a pain than it is worth. They spend so much time looking the word up that it doesn't make sense.

Some spelling tools that we encourage are:

* Word walls that include topical words
* Quick Word Dictionaries that contain only spelling
* Environmental print in texts and in novels
* Word studies
* Friends

Word walls support students as writers because they can quickly and easily pull words from the wall to use in their own writing. As we study words in class, we add them alphabetically to the wall. If, while editing the writing, we see misspellings of words that we have studied, we refer kids to the wall.

Word studies are another effective tool to help kids spell correctly. As a class, we study prefixes and suffixes, learn spelling rules that are consistent, and give examples of everything. As we are studying, we make charts of those words and post them on the wall for kids to access. When we notice the kids looking at the charts, we reward them orally because they are taking control of the spelling process.

Word Lists

Kids really struggle when they are told to edit for spelling. One tangible way to have kids edit is to use their spelling word lists. Of course, it's too much for them to edit a piece of writing for the entire list at one time.

Their word lists are taken directly from their writing much of the time, so this activity reinforces their spelling words. Starting with the first word on the spelling list, they check their entire writing for that word. Every time they encounter the word, they check to see if it's spelled correctly. When they have completed checking the whole writing piece for that word, they put a check next to it on the word list. Then, they edit their entire writing for the second word on the list. This way, they have repeated experience with each word and are working in the context of their own writing. While the spelling list isolates the spelling, editing for those words takes it back to the context of their own writing.

Words that appear on individual word lists include:

* High-frequency words
* Repeatedly misspelled words in a specific text
* Word families (rapidly increases numbers of words that can be spelled correctly)
* Words misspelled by many writers in the room

This also keeps the writer engaged with reading. They are constantly rereading their own writing to look for these words. They are responsible for editing their own work, which reduces the amount I have to edit.

Understanding Different Spellers

There are different types of spellers and their spelling has nothing to do with intelligence. In some cases, spelling ability has nothing to do with how much a person reads. Usually voracious readers can identify misspelled words because they've seen the correct form of the word so often, but this isn't always the case.

The following case studies show three students, each of whom had specific needs as a writer. Nick needed to become a reader before he could become a writer; Liam was a good speller but no one ever knew it because he didn't write; and Marina was a great writer but needed a lot of spelling work.

Nick, Fourth Grade

At the beginning of the year, Nick's writing was almost incomprehensible because of poor handwriting and spelling. He rarely read and definitely despised writing. In class conversations, his verbal skills were amazing. He knew so much more than he could get down on paper. He was the kind of kid who verbally went to the heart of his topic and drew parallels to his own life and life around him.

When Nick did read, he selected books in Osbourne's *Magic Treehouse* series and was bored. His miscue analysis in those books was at the independent level, so I pushed him to tackle harder text with complex story lines. Gary Paulsen's *Mr. Tucket* books were the key to Nick's reading. Miscue analysis in that text was on the verge between independent and instructional. Nick was one of those overnight success stories (man, we love that!) and became a voracious reader. He read *Harris and Me* and *Hatchet*, and then went on to *Old Yeller* and *Where the Red Fern Grows* in another month.

On his own, Nick began to imitate Paulsen's style in his writing. Nick began to experiment with poetry in his Living Book and received lots of support from his peers. He began to like to write.

We had a breakthrough with his writing when he was given an article about the sage grouse in Colorado. The sage grouse was suffering rapidly decreasing numbers due to habitat loss and, believe it or not, the West Nile virus. The virus was killing grouse in unprecedented numbers and wildlife officials were worried. Nick got excited about this topic, and his writing changed. He did research and wrote to present his ideas to other classes. He was engaged and motivated for the first time.

Several months later, there was a noticeable difference in his spelling. In a conference, it became obvious that basic words were spelled correctly and that misspelled words were close approximations. He didn't appeal to me for help with spelling anymore and was able to solve his issues by using the Quick Word Dictionary and by referring to his research for correctly spelled words.

He could explain why he made choices about his spelling and talked about visualizing words from the novels he had been reading. He would try writing the words and then check to see if they matched what he knew looked right.

His spelling changed because he had a purpose for writing; he needed to communicate with his audience. His newfound love of reading and writing had solved his spelling issues. His spelling struggles were more an issue of motivation than ability.

We worked to build Nick's spelling vocabulary because his vocabulary didn't match his oral language. He was still a little leery of unknown words after years of spelling struggles and feelings of inadequacy. One danger, though, is that now that he's having spelling success, he's playing it safe and sticking to known words rather than risking harder vocabulary words.

Liam, Third Grade

Liam was an extremely introverted student. He didn't speak in school until the middle of second grade and there had been talk of retention because of academics. Liam's writing at the beginning of third grade was a mess. I could barely read the handwriting, and his ideas were undeveloped and made no sense. He didn't tie ideas together and the purpose behind the writing was rarely discernible. He hated writing, and his acting-out behavior escalated during writing in an attempt to get kicked out of class. He was all about avoidance.

Imagine my surprise when I realized that his spelling was almost flawless. Once I waded through his handwriting and got over the fact that the writing made no sense, I realized that Liam rarely made spelling errors. Liam needs little spelling support but needs all kinds of advance organizers and conferences to help him organize thinking before writing and to produce more of it. He needs constant checks during the class period to keep him on track.

Liam is a visual kid. He gets a lot of support from classmates because his drawing is gorgeous and detailed. He loves Egypt and constantly is drawing Pharaohs, tombs, and Egyptian artifacts. The first step was to get him writing about Egypt. That helped, but it wasn't the total answer. He became more engaged and excited, but writing was still a challenge.

I worked to help Liam develop a more extensive vocabulary, especially words needed for nonfiction writing. I was curious, given his oral language development, to see if his vocabulary was limiting his verbalization of ideas and was part of the reason he didn't like to write. Liam was like a rose. As his personality unfolded, so did the writing. His writing improved dramatically and his spelling stayed consistently accurate.

Marina, Fourth Grade

Marina is a gifted writer. She willingly shares her Living Book and her manuscripts and receives abundant support from her peers. Her classmates identify Marina as one of the best writers in the room, and the class looks forward to hearing her read her writing. She can take a mundane topic and add drama and excitement in a way that makes everyone wish they had written about the same topic.

She is an avid reader who always has her nose buried in a book. She delights in books, comparing her own writing to that of other authors and using their techniques in her own writing.

Marina is an awful speller, and it is frustrating for her. Poor spelling does not inhibit her writing, but it is painful for her because she realizes her spelling keeps readers away or at least at a distance.

Marina is motivated to improve her spelling. She has improved to the point that she can identify about 80 percent of misspelled words in her writing, which is exciting. With Marina, if the teacher scaffolds instruction with missed words, she can usually identify the correct spelling. For example, if she spelled "challenge" as "challage," we look at what how she has spelled it, then we write what she has done correctly and leave blanks for corrections:

Misspelled word	Scaffold	Second attempt
challage	*chall_ _ge*	*challenge*

Marina sounds out the phonemes and then tries the word a second time. Usually she gets the word right, which indicates that she is noticing patterns and is improving as a speller.

Marina joined a spelling invitational group and we worked on spelling patterns, getting as many words into her spelling vocabulary as possible. If she had misspelled high-frequency words in her writing, words that have many related words, we studied them to reduce the number of words incorrectly spelled in her writing. For example, if she missed *fight*, when she learned the correct spelling, she could then spell all other words that are part of that pattern. Therefore, she also has *light, might, night, right, sight,* and *tight*. She also studied words with the same sound but a different spelling. So, her list also included words like *bite* and *kite*.

Some tips for spelling invitational groups are:

* Keep groups small.
* Organize kids with like needs into one group.
* Create groups with partners in mind so they can be paired to work together.
* Limit words to reinforce the process first; add words later.

Clearly, each writer has specific needs in spelling. Conferences and invitational groups work to satisfy those needs.

The Point of Punctuation

A small town between Dayton and Cincinnati, Ohio, received a lot of press years ago with the addition of a punctuation mark to its name. Driving south on I-75, there was little to distinguish this town from all the others when viewed from the freeway until somebody decided to add an exclamation mark to the name.

Suddenly Hamilton! garnered all kinds of attention and acclaim—not for quality of life or incredible schools or beautiful parks, but for a lowly punctuation mark. Nothing else changed about the town. When getting ready for weekend outings, we didn't suddenly proclaim, "Let's go to Hamilton! I hear it's really a happening place!" Hamilton! was still Hamilton, after all.

Punctuation aids comprehension and expression of meaning. If a writer cannot properly punctuate, it blocks the intended message. A couple of years ago, I read a starkly beautiful book called *Plainsong* by Kent Haruf. It is a simple account of people living in a small prairie town in Colorado. The writing is spare and simple, like the title, which refers to singing in churches before the arrival of organs on the prairie.

What threw me for the first four or five chapters was the lack of quotation marks. I constantly had to reread to determine what was spoken, what was inferred, and what was both. This frustrating experience validated the importance of punctuation and its role in comprehension. While the lack of quotation marks made the first chapters difficult, it suited the style of the book, but it made punctuation conventions very important to understanding the text.

As with spelling, students who read widely tend to be able to punctuate writing properly because they see it in print. The more students read and pay attention to conventions of print, the quicker they learn the conventions.

It's important that the teacher consistently model the conventions in writing. While modeling the thinking in writing demonstrations, the teacher should point out the punctuation and the purpose it serves. It might help to provide time for students to talk about why the punctuation was used in the way that it was and to experiment with other ways to punctuate the piece.

Janet Angelillo's book, *A Fresh Approach to Teaching Punctuation* (2002) is very insightful. She states, "Teachers need to provide direct instruction in written conventions, but that instruction should be part of a sustained, larger inquiry . . . Random lessons that pop up here and there do not make as much sense to children, because the lessons have no context. A study over several weeks, or a string of mini-lessons over several days, helps children settle into new learning and create a mental picture to place it on" (p. 33).

Angelillo places students into small study groups. Each group takes one punctuation mark to study and research over a period of days. The goal of the study group is to come up with a definition of the punctuation mark it's studying and then find examples from a text to illustrate that convention's use. The students study the author's uses of the punctuation, and they explore how they might use it in their own writing.

This approach puts the responsibility on the shoulders of each group, with the teacher's direction. It's constructivist instead of being delivered by the teacher. It is reading based, requiring the students to use text to find examples to illustrate the punctuation mark.

One concern might be that by breaking the class into teams that study specific marks, they will all become experts with one punctuation mark but won't master the others. Learning from other kids in the class might not provide the immersion and time with other punctuation marks to truly internalize the learning.

Most kids seem to use basic punctuation marks fairly consistently, even when they do so incorrectly. To differentiate instruction according to which punctuation marks kids have internalized in order to place them into study groups, a teacher can review writing pieces that have not been edited. Placement is critical so that students will be challenged but not overwhelmed. If they are challenged, it will increase their engagement, as long as the challenge is manageable.

Based on assessments of the writing in my room, the following needed a lot of work:

* Commas in a series
* Punctuation in quotes

* Exclamation points and question marks to vary writing
* Punctuation for names of towns, countries, and so on

Kids who struggle with writing as a whole tend to be inconsistent in their use of the basic period, question mark, and exclamation point. They need a chance to study these marks a bit more. Other students know and use basic marks consistently and are ready for the challenges that harder marks would make on their writing. Some writers have the conventions down and are proficient at using correct punctuation, but their writing is dull and flat. The study of harder punctuation marks might lead them to write more complex pieces if they are also approximating what great writers do in their writing. For example, we might look at Gary Paulsen's use of sentence fragments and punctuation to create suspense, and they might imitate his punctuation style in their writing.

Surprisingly, some of the more sophisticated writers aren't consistent with the basic marks. They write thoughtfully, have complex story lines, and describe multilayered characters and events that would benefit from more complex punctuation marks. These students need to struggle with quotation marks, colons, ellipses, and semicolons so that their writing can be complex and clear at the same time. However, some of our Charlotte Brontës and Cynthia Rylants don't have a good handle on the more basic punctuation marks yet!

The options are to place them in a basic punctuation study or in a more advanced study of complex marks. To place those writers in a basic punctuation group would deny them the learning they need to improve their writing. Their punctuation problems may be more an editing issue than a knowledge issue. These writers may be so intent on their message that they don't take the time to edit and apply the punctuation that they truly know. It's almost as if they are so busy creating beautiful writing that they can't be bothered with the mundane necessities of writing. If this is the case, these kids would benefit from some time on editing and editing check sheets, which would get them into learning what they really need as writers.

Here are some thoughts on organizing a classroom punctuation inquiry study:

* Limit the number of punctuation marks being studied.
* Assign several groups to one punctuation mark.
* Keep groups small to increase engagement.

* Model how charts may look.
* Use a variety of texts to increase applicability.
* Encourage quoting novels.

To begin our classroom study, I limited study groups to three topics: a basic punctuation study group, a group that would investigate quotation marks, and a group that studied ellipses.

Surprisingly, after the purpose of the groups was outlined and the kids selected which groups they thought they should work with, twenty-two of them made the same choice I would have made for them. Only one kid chose a more complicated study group than he belonged in.

I allowed more than twenty minutes per day for two solid weeks for the punctuation groups to meet. My role during this study was to support the learning in the classroom, facilitate students' reflections, help students with their examples and with placing those examples on charts, and work with the groups on planning how they would present the learned information to the rest of the class.

The punctuation studies groups increased engagement in spelling and punctuation. The students became more aware of punctuation marks, and they began to enjoy playing with them.

Angelillo (2002) discusses the role of reading in helping kids "hear" punctuation as well as other techniques to help kids internalize correct use of punctuation. She considers punctuation on an emotional level, too, talking about its beauty and the impact that punctuation marks make on the meaning. The "About the Author" section of her book says that she lives in New York City, but I'm sure she must have been born in Hamilton!

Epilogue

Of Life Mentors and Lack of Original Thought

Ellin Keene was the featured speaker at an in-service in our district. It was a return to her roots because she had taught in our district for many years in various capacities. In addition, she had worked extensively at our school (Castle Rock Elementary School) the previous year helping to extend our literacy thinking.

She was coming home, like Evita returning to Argentina, only there was no cool music. We, her groupies, packed the front rows, anxiously awaiting our mentor who had given so freely of herself. We were excited too, because after every interaction with Ellin, our literacy understandings exploded, so we knew this in-service would be great.

As she gazed out at the crowd of teachers assembled before her, it was clear she was nervous. She began graciously and eloquently, as always. Suddenly, we were electrified. Ellin was sharing with us her latest thinking, new thinking on teaching writing. She was taking a risk in front of colleagues.

Instead of reading comprehension strategy work, she began by talking about the qualities of effective writing process classrooms and our role in those classrooms. She reinforced, time and again, the critical need to model our thinking, writing process issues, and reading comprehension strategies because of the impact of that modeling on students' growth.

Repeatedly, she stressed the need for student self-selection of topics to increase engagement. Equally important was the need to embed, within those self-selected topics, our teaching of language conventions. Further, to increase internalization and application of those conventions we were teaching, students needed real audiences to increase the engagement during the writing process.

She envisioned rooms that surrounded and immersed students in beautiful text, eloquent writing, and passionate works of art from the masters. Instead of immeasurable time spent on test preparation, our time would be better spent inspecting and analyzing works of art, both painted and printed, seeking to emulate these masterpieces, to produce something of stature. For this to happen, students needed a warm, safe environment in which to take risks.

The audience buzzed. What was she doing? This was an in-service. In a culture where test preparation, standards, and bodies-of-evidence hysteria reigned supreme, this bordered on blasphemy. Where was the talk of graphic organizers, three-sentence paragraphs, and transitional clauses? What about piloting the new standards-based report card? Was she going to talk about going online to access the reporting procedures? What was happening here? Someone whispered, "She's talking about *teaching*!" The audience sat up and began scribbling notes furiously.

Then she went to the heart of her writing beliefs—that we need to be writers ourselves so that we can understand the life of a writer, that we need to share our writing with our students and model our techniques and conventions of print, that this is how we will create trust and intimacy in our classrooms and bring our learning to them. That is, if we explore our ideas in writing, we might create a deeper understanding of our life and the world around us.

The audience resembled more of a church revival in southern Ohio than a district in-service. It got more boisterous as she spoke of passion, passion for our lives and passion for the writing that allows us to explore our lives. She spoke of our need to create something of lasting beauty.

Audience behavior went from tent revival to a Bronco vs. Raiders football game. People were standing up and applauding. They were talking excitedly to each other, throwing out comments and ideas. And then she said the simple words that went right to our hearts. "We need to leave something luminous, something that matters in the world." Our role is to inspire others by being passionate learners, to push the limits of our own learning, and to create beauty in our classrooms, and moreover, to expect every child, every student to create beauty, too.

People began cheering and gave her a standing ovation.

Ellin is a model of courage in a time when teachers need it badly. Our jobs as teachers are incredibly difficult. The challenge inspires me. But, honestly, some days I could use a little less challenge!

It's awesome that so many teachers find the courage within themselves to go on, to make their mark, to leave "something luminous." The Sheris, the Pats and Dans, the Carens and Shirleys, the Dawns, the Barbs and Debs and Marlas and Tamis and Carolyns, the Amys. These are the teachers who help make the ideas of working with tween writers from mentors like Ellin come to life in my classroom.

Our roles in the lives of our students are giant. And every day, we have yet another chance to make it right, to make that contact, to make a connection, to love, to be loved. For many tweens, it's our humanness, our passion for life, our ability to forgive and move on, that will influence their lives most profoundly.

I hope that as students come to us and leave us, part of that shared living will be documented in writing. Forever.

Appendix

Brian Cambourne's Conditions of Learning

Strategy:

* Immersion

* Demonstration (see Planning)

* Expectations

* Responsibility

* Employment

* Approximation

* Response

Writing Through the Tween Years: Supporting Writers, Grades 3–6 by Bruce Morgan with Deb Odom. Copyright © 2005. Stenhouse Publishers.

Writing Crafting Lessons

Date	Writing Crafting	Reflection

Writing Invitational Groups

Participants	Focus	Provider	Resource

Writing Through the Tween Years: Supporting Writers, Grades 3–6 by Bruce Morgan with Deb Odom. Copyright © 2005. Stenhouse Publishers.

Reading Crafting Lessons

Date	Reading Crafting	Reflection

Reading Invitational Groups

Participants	Focus	Provider	Resource

Reading Check-In

Name	Text	Mon.	Tues.	Wed.	Thurs.	Fri.

Strategies Used by Proficient Learners

Ellin Keene

Determine What Is Important in Text

Readers
* Readers identify key ideas or themes as they read.
* Readers distinguish important from unimportant information in relation to key ideas or themes in text. They can distinguish important information at the word, sentence, and text level.
* Readers use text structure and text features (such as bold or italicized print, figures, and photographs) to help them distinguish important from unimportant information.
* Readers use their knowledge of important and relevant parts of text to prioritize in long-term memory and synthesize text for others.

Writers
* Writers observe their world and record what they believe is significant.
* Writers make decisions about the most important ideas to include in the pieces they write. They make decisions about the best genre and structure to communicate their ideas.
* Writers reveal their biases by emphasizing some elements.
* Writers provide only essential detail to reveal the meaning and produce the desired effect.
* Writers delete information irrelevant to their larger purpose.

Draw Inferences

Readers
* Readers use their schema and textual information to draw conclusions and interpret text.
* Readers make predictions about text, confirm their predictions, and test their developing meaning as they read.
* Readers know when and how to use text in combination with their own background knowledge to seek answers to questions.
* Readers create interpretations to enrich and deepen their experience of a text.

Writers
* Writers make decisions about content inclusions/exclusions and genre/text structure that permit or encourage inference on the part of the reader.
* Writers carefully consider their audience in making decisions about what to describe explicitly and what to leave to the reader's interpretation.

Writing Through the Tween Years: Supporting Writers, Grades 3–6 by Bruce Morgan with Deb Odom. Copyright © 2005. Stenhouse Publishers.

* Writers, particularly fiction and poetry writers, are aware of far more detail than they reveal in the texts they compose. This encourages readers to infer by drawing conclusions, making critical judgments, predicting, and connecting to other texts and experiences.

Use Prior Knowledge (Schema)

Readers
* Readers spontaneously activate relevant, prior knowledge before, during, and after reading text.
* Readers assimilate information from text into their schemata and make changes in that schemata to accommodate the new information.
* Readers use schema to relate text to their world knowledge, textual knowledge, and personal experience.
* Readers use their schema to enhance their understanding of text and to store textual information in long-term memory.
* Readers use their schema for authors and their styles to understand text.
* Readers recognize when they have inadequate background information and know how to create it—to build schema—to get the information they need.

Writers
* Writers frequently choose their topics and write about subjects they care about.
* A writer's content comes from and builds on his or her experiences.
* Writers think about and use what they know about genre, text structure, and conventions as they write.
* Writers seek to better recognize and capitalize on their own voice for specific effects in their compositions.
* Writers know when their schema for a topic or text format is inadequate and they create the necessary background knowledge.
* Writers use knowledge of their audience to decide what to include and exclude.

Ask Questions

Readers
* Readers spontaneously generate questions before, during, and after reading.
* Readers ask questions for different purposes including to clarify meaning; make predictions; determine an author's style, content, or format; locate a specific answer in text; and consider rhetorical questions inspired by the text.
* Readers use questions to focus their attention on important components of the text.

Writing Through the Tween Years: Supporting Writers, Grades 3–6 by Bruce Morgan with Deb Odom. Copyright © 2005. Stenhouse Publishers.

* Readers are aware that other readers' questions may inspire new questions for them.

Writers
* Writers compose in a way that causes the reader to form question as they read.
* Writers monitor their progress by asking questions about their choices as they write.
* Writers ask questions of other writers in order to confirm their choices and make revisions.
* Writers' questions lead to revision in their own pieces and in the pieces to which they respond for other writers.

Monitor Meaning and Comprehension

Readers
* Readers monitor their comprehension during reading. They know when the text they are reading or listening to makes sense, when it does not, what does not make sense, and whether the unclear portions are critical to overall understanding of the piece.
* Readers can identify when text is comprehensible and the degree to which they understand it. They can identify ways in which a text becomes gradually more understandable by reading past an unclear portion and/or by rereading parts or all of the text.
* Readers are aware of the processes they can use to make meaning clear. They check, evaluate, and revise their evolving interpretation of the text while reading.
* Readers can identify confusing ideas, themes, and/or surface elements (words, sentence, text structures, graphs, tables, etc.) and can suggest a variety of means to solve the problems they have.
* Readers are aware of what they *need* to comprehend in relation to their purpose for reading.
* Readers must *learn* how to pause, consider the meanings in text, reflect on their understandings, and use different strategies to enhance their understanding. This process is best learned by watching proficient models "think-aloud" and gradually taking responsibility for monitoring their own comprehension as they read independently.

Writers
* Writers monitor their composition process to ensure that their text makes sense for their intended audience at the word, sentence, and text level.
* Writers read their work aloud to find and hear their voice.
* Writers share their work so others can help them monitor the clarity and impact of the work.
* Writers pay attention to their style and purpose. They purposefully

Writing Through the Tween Years: Supporting Writers, Grades 3–6 by Bruce Morgan with Deb Odom. Copyright © 2005. Stenhouse Publishers.

write with clarity and honesty. They strive to write boldly, simply, and concisely by keeping those standards alive in their minds during the writing process.

* Writers pause to consider the impact of their work and make conscious decisions about when to turn a small piece into a larger project, when revisions are complete, or when to abandon a piece.

Fix-Up Strategies

Readers

* Readers use the six major systems of language (grapho-phonic, lexical, syntactic, semantic, schematic, and pragmatic) to solve reading problems. When not comprehending, they ask themselves questions such as, Does this make sense? Does the word I'm pronouncing sound like language? Do the letters in the word match the sounds I'm pronouncing? Have I seen this word before? Is there another reader who can help me make sense of this? What do I already know from my experience and the context of this text that can help me solve this problem?

* Readers have and select a wide range of problem-solving strategies and can make appropriate choices in a given reading situation (i.e., skip ahead or reread, use the context and syntax, sound it out, speak to another reader, consider relevant prior knowledge, read the passage aloud, etc.).

Writers

* Writers revise (add, delete, and reorganize) and edit (apply correct conventions), continually seeking clarity and impact for the reader. They experiment with and change overall meaning, content, wording, text organization, punctuation, and spelling.

* Writers capitalize on their knowledge of writers' tools (i.e., character, setting, conflict, theme, plot structure, leads, style, etc.) to enhance their meaning.

Synthesize Information

Readers

* Readers maintain a cognitive synthesis as they read. They monitor the overall meaning, important concepts, and themes in the text as they read and are aware of ways text elements "fit together" to create that overall meaning and theme. They use their knowledge of these elements to decide on the overall meaning of a passage, chapter, or book.

* Readers retell or synthesize what they have read. They attend to the most important information and to the clarity or the synthesis itself. Readers synthesize to understand what they have read.

* Readers capitalize on opportunities to share, recommend, and criticize books they have read.

* Readers respond to text in a variety or ways, independently or in groups of other readers. These include written, oral, dramatic, and artistic responses and interpretations of text.
* A proficient reader's synthesis is likely to extend the literal meaning of a text to the inferential level.

Writers
* Writers make global and focal plans for their writing before and during the drafting process. They use their knowledge of text elements such as character, setting, conflict, sequence of events, and resolution to create a structure for their writing.
* Writers study other writers and draw conclusions about what makes good writing. They work to replicate the style of authors they find compelling.
* Writers reveal themes in a way that suggests their importance to readers. Readers can create a cogent synthesis from well-written material.

Use Sensory Images

Readers
* Readers create sensory images during and after reading. These images may include visual, auditory, and other sensory as well as emotional connections to the text and are rooted in prior knowledge.
* Readers use images to draw conclusions about and to interpret the text. Images from reading frequently become part of the reader's writing. Images from a reader's personal experience frequently become part of their comprehension.
* Readers use their images to clarify and enhance comprehension.
* Readers use images to immerse themselves in rich detail as they read. The detail gives depth and dimension to the reading, engaging the reader more deeply and making the text more memorable.
* Readers adapt their images in response to the shared images of other readers.
* Readers adapt their images as they continue to read. Images are revised to incorporate new information revealed through the text and new interpretations as they are developed by the reader.

Writers
* Writers consciously attempt to create strong images in their compositions using strategically placed detail.
* Writers create impact through the use of strong nouns and verbs whenever possible.
* Writers use images to explore their ideas. They consciously study their mental images for direction in their pieces.
* Writers learn from the images created in their minds as they read. They study other authors' use of images as a way to improve their own.

Writing Through the Tween Years: Supporting Writers, Grades 3–6 by Bruce Morgan with Deb Odom. Copyright © 2005. Stenhouse Publishers.

References

Angelillo, Janet. 2002. *A Fresh Approach to Teaching Punctuation*. New York: Scholastic.

Babbitt, Natalie. 1986. *Tuck Everlasting*. New York: Farrar Straus Giroux.

Bunting, Eve. 1989. *Terrible Things*. New York: Jewish Society of America.

———. 1998. *So Far from the Sea*. New York: Clarion.

———. 1999. *Smoky Nights*. New York: Voyager.

———. 2003. *Cheyenne Again*. New York: Sagebrush.

Calkins, Lucy. 1998. *A Teacher's Guide to Standardized Reading Tests*. Portsmouth, NH: Heinemann.

Cambourne, Brian. 1993. *The Whole Story*. New York: Scholastic.

Chandler, Kelly, and the Mapleton Teacher-Research Group. 1999. *Spelling Inquiry: How One Elementary School Caught the Mnemonic Plague*. Portland, ME: Stenhouse.

Cisneros, Sandra. 1991. *The House on Mango Street*. New York: Vintage.

Clements, Andrew. 2004. *Things Not Seen*. New York: Puffin.

Creech, Sharon. 1996. *Walk Two Moons*. New York: HarperTrophy.

dePaola, Tomie. 1981. *Now One Foot, Now the Other*. New York: Putnam.

Culham, Ruth. 2003. *6 + 1 Traits of Writing*. New York: Scholastic.

DiCamillo, Kate. 2001. *Because of Winn-Dixie*. Cambridge, MA: Candlewick.

Fox, Mem. 1985. *Wilfrid Gordon McDonald Partridge*. La Jolla, CA: Kane/Miller.

Gentry, J. Richard. 1989. *Spel . . . Is a Four-Letter Word*. Portsmouth, NH: Heinemann.

Gipson, Fred. 2004. *Old Yeller*. New York: HarperTrophy.

Haruf, Kent. 2000. *Plainsong*. New York: Vintage.

Hindley, Joanne. 1996. *In the Company of Children*. Portland, ME: Stenhouse.

Hulbert, Ann. 2003. "Tween-Age Wasteland." August 29.

Keene, Ellin, and Susan Zimmermann. 1997. *Mosaic of Thought: Teaching Comprehension in a Reader's Workshop*. Portsmouth, NH: Heinemann.

Lee, Harper. 1999. *To Kill a Mockingbird*. New York: Little, Brown.

Lollis, Sylvia. 2002. *Should We Have Pets?* New York: Mondo.

Lyons, Carol. 2003. *Teaching Struggling Readers: How to Use Brain-Based Research to Maximize Learning*. Portsmouth, NH: Heinemann.

MacLachlan, Patricia. 1995. *Baby*. New York: Yearling.

———. 1998. *What You Know First*. New York: HarperTrophy.

Miller, Debbie. 2002. *Reading with Meaning: Teaching Comprehension in the Primary Grades*. Portland, ME: Stenhouse.

Mochizuki, Ken. 1997. *Passage to Freedom: The Sugihara Story*. New York: Lee & Low.

Newkirk, Thomas. 2002. *Misreading Masculinity: Boys, Literacy, and Popular Culture*. Portsmouth, NH: Heinemann.

O'Dell, Scott. 1988. *Streams to the River, Rivers to the Sea*. New York: Fawcett.

———. 1997. *Sing Down the Moon*. New York: Laurel-Leaf.

Park, Barbara. 1996. *Mick Harte Was Here*. New York: Random House.

Paulsen, Gary. 1995. *Harris and Me*. New York: Yearling.

———. 2000. *Hatchet*. New York: Atheneum.

Pearson, David, and Margaret Gallagher. 1983. "The Instruction of Reading Comprehension." *Contemporary Educational Psychology* 8: 317–344.

Rawls, Wilson. 1984. *Where the Red Fern Grows*. New York: Random House.

Rylant, Cynthia. 1985. *When I Was Young in the Mountains*. New York: Dutton.

———. 1991. *Night in the Country*. New York: Aladdin.

———. 1993. *The Relatives Came*. New York: Aladdin.

———. 1996a. *An Angel for Solomon Singer*. New York: Orchard.

———. 1996b. *The Old Woman Who Named Things*. New York: Harcourt.

———. 2001. *Scarecrow*. New York: Voyager.

Sachar, Louis. 2000. *Holes*. New York: Yearling.

Slate. http://slate.msn.com/id/2087714/

Smith, Michael, and Jeffrey D. Wilhelm. 2002. *"Reading Don't Fix No Chevy's": Literacy in the Lives of Young Men*. Portsmouth, NH: Heinemann.

Spinelli, Jerry. 2002. *Stargirl*. New York: Knopf.

Stead, Tony. 2002. *Should There Be Zoos?* New York: Mondo.

Thomasma, Kenneth. 1983. *Naya Nuki*. Grand Rapids, MI: Baker Book House.

———. 1984. *Soun Tetoken*. Grand Rapids, MI: Baker Book House.

———. 2000. *Om-Kas-Toe*. Bellevue, WA: Grandview.

Tsuchiya, Yukio. 1988. *Faithful Elephants*. Boston: Houghton Mifflin.

Van Allsburg, Chris. 1986. *The Stranger*. Boston: Houghton Mifflin.

Viorst, Judith. 1999. *The Tenth Best Thing About Barney*. New York: Aladdin.

Williams, Jackie Napolean. 2002. *Hidden Witness*. New York: St. Martin's.

Zolotow, Charlotte. 1992. *The Seashore Book*. New York: HarperCollins.

Series Books

MacLachlan, Patricia. *Sarah, Plain and Tall* trilogy.

Osbourne, Mary Pope. *Magic Treehouse*.

Paulsen, Gary. *Mr. Tucket*.

Wilder, Laura Ingalls. *Little House on the Prairie*.